JAMESTOWN  EDUCATION

The Outer Edge™
Uncommon Courage

Henry Billings
Melissa Billings

 Glencoe

New York, New York   Columbus, Ohio   Chicago, Illinois   Peoria, Illinois   Woodland Hills, California

 JAMESTOWN EDUCATION

Reviewers

Kati Pearson
Literacy Coordinator
Carver Middle School
4500 West Columbia Street
Orlando, FL 32811

Suzanne Zweig
Reading Specialist
Sullivan High School
6631 North Bosworth Avenue
Chicago, IL 60626

Beth Dalton
Reading Consultant
Los Angeles County Office of
Education
9300 Imperial Avenue
Downey, CA 90240

Carolyn S. Reid
Reading Specialist
Alief Hastings High School
12301 High Star
Houston, TX 77072

 **Glencoe**

The **McGraw·Hill** Companies

ISBN: 0-07-872904-1

Send all queries to:
Glencoe/McGraw-Hill
8787 Orion Place
Columbus, OH 43240-4027

3 4 5 6 7 8 9   024   09 08 07 06

Contents

Unit Three

To the Student

Everyday people do things that take courage. Once in a while, someone faces a task that calls for a great deal of courage. Uncommon courage can take many forms. It can mean standing up for what you believe in. It can mean risking your own life. It can mean suffering great pain. There are 13 true stories in this book. In them you will meet people who show uncommon courage in the face of danger.

As you do the lessons in this book, you will improve your reading skills. This will help you increase your reading comprehension. You also will improve your thinking skills. The lessons include types of questions often found on state and national tests. Working with these questions will help you prepare for tests you may have to take in the future.

How to Use This Book

About the Book.   *Uncommon Courage* has three units. Each one has four lessons. Each lesson starts with a true story. The stories are about people who show courage in the face of danger. Each story is followed by a group of seven exercises. They test comprehension and thinking skills. They will help you understand and think about what you read. At the end of the lesson, you can give your personal response. You can also rate how well you understood what you read.

The Sample Lesson.   The first lesson in the book is a sample. It explains how to complete the questions. It also shows how to score your answers. The correct answers are printed in lighter type. In some cases, the reasons an answer is correct are given. Studying these reasons will help you learn how to think through the questions. You might have questions about how to do the exercises or score them. If so, you should ask those questions now, before you start Unit One.

Working Through Each Lesson.   Start each lesson by looking at the photo. Next read the caption. Before you read the story, guess what you think it will be about. Then read the story.

After you finish the story, do the exercises. Study the directions for each exercise. They will tell you how to mark your answers. Do all seven exercises. Then check your work. Your teacher will give you an answer key to do this. Follow the directions after each exercise to find your score. At the end of the lesson, add up your total score. Record that score on the graph on page 115.

At the end of each unit, you will complete a Compare and Contrast Chart. The chart will help you see what some of the stories in that unit have in common. It will also help you explore your own ideas about the events in the stories.

SAMPLE LESSON

The Heroes of Flight 93

The people on Flight 93 were in big trouble. But they did not know it yet. At 9:25 A.M. on September 11, 2001, most of them had settled in for a long flight. They had just left New Jersey. They were not expected to reach California for hours. They didn't know that their lives—and the lives of many others—were in terrible danger.

2 That day, terrorists attacked the United States. The terrorists took over three planes. They crashed two into the two towers of the World Trade Center in New York City. They flew the third straight into the Pentagon. (The Pentagon is an important government building in Washington, D.C.) Now four more terrorists sat on Flight 93. They planned to take over this plane too.

3 The terrorists pulled out red scarves. They tied them to their heads. Then they moved forward. They forced their way into the cockpit. Using box cutters as knives, they hurt or killed two of the crew. In minutes, they took charge of the plane.

4 The passengers were terrified. They thought the men had a bomb. Some passengers pulled out their cell phones. They called home to say goodbye to their loved ones. During these calls, they heard about the other plane crashes. Word spread quickly through the plane. Soon everyone knew what was going on. The terrorists planned to kill them all. They planned to fly the plane into some important building on the East Coast.

5 This news could not have been worse. The people on Flight 93 now knew that their lives were about to end. No one would have blamed them if they just gave up. After all, what could they do? The men in the red scarves seemed to have all the power.

6 But the passengers did not see it that way. They vowed not to go down without a fight. They hoped to win back control of the plane. They knew their chances were not good. But even if they failed, they could at least keep the plane from hitting its target.

7 And so they tried to control their fears. Talking softly, they began to make plans. The terrorists must have sensed something. They told people to move to the back of the plane. Moving back was fine with crew member Sandy Bradshaw. It put her close to the plane's kitchen. On her cell phone, she told her husband she was going to use a coffeepot as a weapon. "We are here in the back trying to get hot water to throw on them," she said.

8 Tom Burnett called his wife, Deena. "We're going to do something," he told her.

This wreath was made to honor the people who died on Flight 93.

9 "Tom," she cried, "sit down. Be still. Be quiet. Don't draw attention to yourself." She hoped that someone in charge would step in and take back the plane.

10 But Tom knew that would not happen. "We can't wait, Deena," he told her. "If they are going to run this plane into the ground, we're going to do something."

11 Jeremy Glick felt the same way. He and Mark Bingham also made final phone calls to their families. "It doesn't look good," Bingham said. He also said, "In case I don't see you again, I love you all." Glick told his wife that the passengers had taken a vote. They had agreed to attack the terrorists.

12 Todd Beamer could not reach his family. Instead, he got through to a phone company official. Her name was Lisa Jefferson. Beamer asked her to tell his wife and sons that he loved them. Then he told Jefferson of the plans to make a run at the terrorists.

13 "Are you sure that's what you want to do, Todd?" Jefferson asked him.

14 "It's what we have to do," he said. Beamer began to pray. Jefferson joined in. Then Jefferson heard Beamer say, "Are you guys ready? Let's roll."

15 "They're doing it! They're doing it!" crew member CeeCee Lyles told her husband over the phone.

16 "I've got to go," Elizabeth Wainio said, ending her phone call to her stepmother. "They're breaking into the cockpit. I love you. Goodbye."

17 No one will ever know just what happened next. The flight recorder picked up some sounds. Dishes crashed. Trays fell. A man screamed. From the ground, people saw the big plane rock from side to side. Then it fell from the sky.

18 No one survived the crash. The four terrorists died. So did the passengers and crew. But the plane did not reach its target. The terrorists had most likely been aiming for the White House or the Capitol. If the plane had crashed there, the loss of life would have been enormous. Hundreds of people would have died. Many leaders would have been killed. That's what the terrorists wanted. And that's what would have happened if the heroes of Flight 93 had not been so brave. In the darkest moments of their lives, they showed what it means to have uncommon courage.

A | Finding the Main Idea

One statement below tells the main idea of the article. One statement is too general, or too broad. The other statement explains only part of the article; it is too narrow. Label the statements using the following key:

M—Main Idea   B—Too Broad   N—Too Narrow

__M__   1. The passengers and crew on Flight 93 bravely fought terrorists and ruined the terrorists' plans. [This statement is the *main idea*. It tells you that the article is about the passengers and crew on Flight 93 who fought and stopped terrorists.]

__B__   2. The passengers and crew of Flight 93 can truly be called heroes. [This statement is an idea in the article, but it is *too broad*. It does not tell why they are called heroes.]

__N__   3. All the passengers and crew on Flight 93 died when the plane crashed on September 11, 2001. [This statement is true, but it is *too narrow*. It gives only a few facts from the article.]

B | Recalling Facts

How well do you remember the facts in the article? Put an X in the box next to the answer that correctly completes each statement.

1. On September 11, 2001, two planes crashed into
   - ☐ a. the ocean.
   - ☒ b. the World Trade Center.
   - ☐ c. the White House.

2. The terrorists hurt or killed two crew members on Flight 93 using
   - ☐ a. lead pipes.
   - ☐ b. guns.
   - ☒ c. box cutters.

3. After a vote, the passengers decided to
   - ☒ a. attack the terrorists.
   - ☐ b. try to talk the terrorists out of hurting them.
   - ☐ c. wait until someone came to help them.

4. When Flight 93 crashed, everyone
   - ☐ a. except the terrorists died.
   - ☒ b. on the plane was killed.
   - ☐ c. except the crew lived.

Score 4 points for each correct answer.

_____ **Total Score:** Finding the Main Idea

Score 4 points for each correct answer.

_____ **Total Score:** Recalling Facts

C | Making Inferences

When you draw a conclusion that is not directly stated in the text, you are making an inference. Put an X in the box next to the statement that is a correct inference.

1.

☐ a. No one on the planes that crashed into the World Trade Center stood up to the terrorists.

☐ b. None of the terrorists on Flight 93 could speak English.

☒ c. Some of the passengers on Flight 93 were strong men.

2.

☐ a. No one could see the terrorists' faces.

☒ b. The terrorists had planned their attack carefully.

☐ c. The terrorists carried bombs on board.

D | Using Words

Put an X in the box next to the definition below that is closest in meaning to the underlined word.

1. The pilot checked all the dials in the plane's <u>cockpit</u>.

☒ a. the part of the plane where the pilot sits

☐ b. the part of the plane where passengers sit

☐ c. the part of the plane where things are stored

2. The little child felt <u>terrified</u> when the big dog ran toward her. She grabbed her mother's hand and cried.

☐ a. happy

☒ b. scared

☐ c. tired

3. <u>Terrorists</u> attacked the frightened country.

☐ a. people who love danger

☐ b. people who fight for freedom

☒ c. people who scare others

4. Before he left home, the son <u>vowed</u> that he would come back.

☐ a. shouted

☒ b. promised

☐ c. read

Score 4 points for each correct answer.

_____ **Total Score:** Making Inferences

5. The children were glad that their dog <u>survived</u> the house fire.

- ☐ a. spread
- ☒ b. lived through
- ☐ c. were afraid of

6. It took four movers to carry the <u>enormous</u> table up the stairs.

- ☒ a. huge
- ☐ b. old
- ☐ c. wooden

Score 4 points for each correct answer.

_____ **Total Score:** Using Words

E | Author's Approach

Put an X in the box next to the correct answer.

1. The author uses the first sentence of the article to

- ☐ a. describe the inside of the plane.
- ☒ b. make the reader wonder what will happen next.
- ☐ c. compare Flight 93 with other flights.

2. What is the author's purpose in writing this article?

- ☐ a. to get the reader ready to fight terrorists
- ☐ b. to list ways that cell phones can be used
- ☒ c. to tell the reader about some brave people

3. Choose the statement below that best describes the author's opinion in paragraph 18.

- ☒ a. The heroes of Flight 93 showed what true courage is.
- ☐ b. The terror on Flight 93 should be forgotten.
- ☐ c. The people in the White House and the Capitol were not as important as the passengers of Flight 93.

Score 4 points for each correct answer.

_____ **Total Score:** Author's Approach

F Summarizing and Paraphrasing

Put an X in the box next to the correct answer.

1. Which summary says all the important things about the article?

☐ a. The passengers of Flight 93 will be remembered forever. They made a big difference in history. [This summary leaves out most important details.]

☐ b. Terrorists on Flight 93 attacked the crew with sharp box cutters. Passengers decided that they had to fight back. [This summary presents some important details from the article but misses too many others.]

☒ c. Terrorists took over Flight 93 on September 11, 2001. After passengers bravely fought the terrorists, the plane crashed before it reached its target. Everyone aboard died. [This summary says all the most important things.]

2. Which sentence means the same thing as the following sentence? "They had agreed to make a run at the terrorists."

☒ a. They had decided to attack the terrorists. [In this sentence, the phrase *make a run at* is replaced by the word *attack*, which means the same thing.]

☐ b. They had agreed to run around the terrorists.

☐ c. They had decided to do what the terrorists said.

Score 4 points for each correct answer.

_____ **Total Score:** Summarizing and Paraphrasing

G Critical Thinking

Put an X in the box next to the correct answer.

1. Choose the statement below that states an opinion.

☒ a. There should be a police officer on every plane that takes off.

☐ b. Many people on Flight 93 understood how important it was to stop the terrorists.

☐ c. Some people on Flight 93 were willing to fight to save others.

2. From information in the article, you can predict that

☐ a. no one will ever want to ride in a plane again.

☐ b. terrorists will never try to take over a plane again.

☒ c. airlines will check more carefully what passengers may bring onto planes.

3. Jeremy Glick and Tom Burnett were alike because they

☐ a. could not reach their families on cell phones.

☐ b. wanted to wait for someone else to save them.

☒ c. decided to fight the terrorists.

4. What probably was one effect of the fact that some passengers on Flight 93 attacked the terrorists?

☒ a. Flight 93 fell to the earth.

☐ b. Two planes hit the World Trade Center.

☐ c. No one knows for sure what made Flight 93 crash.

5. If you were in charge of an airport, how could you use the information in the article to keep terrorists with knives and guns off planes?

☐ a. I would make airplanes stronger, so they would not fall apart as easily if terrorists attacked.

☒ b. I would check passengers to see if they had knives and guns before they got on the plane.

☐ c. I would make sure that many people onboard every plane had cell phones to call for help.

Score 4 points for each correct answer.

_____ **Total Score:** Critical Thinking

Enter your score for each activity. Add the scores together. Record your total score on the graph on page 115.

_____ Finding the Main Idea

_____ Recalling Facts

_____ Making Inferences

_____ Using Words

_____ Author's Approach

_____ Summarizing and Paraphrasing

_____ Critical Thinking

_____ **Total Score**

Personal Response

I agree with the author because

_____

_____

[Write about one way in which you think the same as the author.]

Self-Assessment

Before reading this article, I already knew _____

_____

_____

[Recall facts about the 911 terrorist attacks that you knew before you read the article.]

Self-Assessment

You can take charge of your own progress. Here are some features to help you focus on your progress in learning reading and thinking skills.

Personal Response and Self-Assessment. These questions help you connect the stories to your life. They help you think about your understanding of what you have read.

Comprehension and Critical Thinking Progress Graph. A graph at the end of the book helps you to keep track of your progress. Check the graph often with your teacher. Together, decide whether you need more work on some skills. What types of skills cause you trouble? Talk with your teacher about ways to work on these.

A sample Progress Graph is shown on the right. The first three lessons have been filled in to show you how to use the graph.

Comprehension and Critical Thinking Progress Graph

Directions: Write your score for each lesson in the box under the number of the lesson. Then put a small X on the line directly above the number of the lesson and across from the score you earned. Chart your progress by drawing a line to connect the Xs.

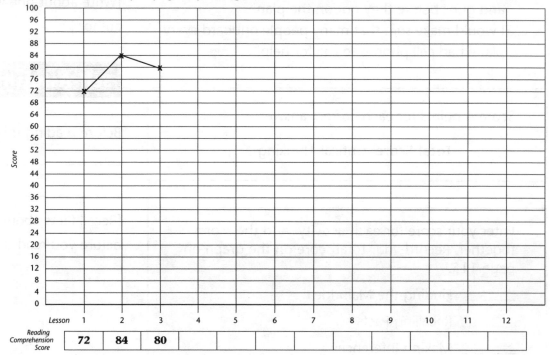

Lesson	1	2	3	4	5	6	7	8	9	10	11	12
Reading Comprehension Score	72	84	80									

UNIT ONE

One Woman's Struggle

Maria Elena Moyano talks to a friendly crowd in Lima, Peru, in 1990.

Maria Elena Moyano knew what it was like to be poor. She was born in Peru in 1958. Her home was just a straw house held up with poles. Her mother washed clothes for rich people. These jobs were hard to find. And they did not pay much. So Moyano's family struggled to survive. "I . . . remember that we were hungry a lot," she said.

2   As Moyano grew up, she dreamed of a better life. She wanted to improve things not just for herself but for the millions of poor people in her country. How could she do this? In the early 1980s, Moyano found a way. By this time, she was married. She had a small child. So she joined a "mothers' club." That helped her meet other women. She and her friends drew up plans. Then they took action. They picked up garbage on their streets. They taught people to boil water so it would be safe to drink. And they set up family kitchens where people could share food. That way all families—even the poorest ones—could get a decent meal.

3   Moyano helped set up hundreds of programs. The biggest one was the Glass of Milk program. Before it started, most poor children went to school with just a cup of tea for breakfast. They had nothing for lunch. At night they might have a few pieces of raw fish. The Glass of Milk program tried to give each child at least one glass of milk a day. The program was a huge success. Soon it was serving more than a million children.

4   By this time, Moyano was quite famous. Most people loved her. But a few hated her. Her enemies came from a group called the Shining Path. At first Moyano had liked this group. Its leaders said that they, too, wished to help the poor. But she soon learned the truth. Shining Path had a bad side. Its leaders wanted power. They would do anything to get it. They killed those who spoke out against them. From 1980 to the present, they killed more than 30,000 people.

5   Moyano knew she could not work with this group. She hated violence. In September 1991, the Shining Path killed a friend of hers. This woman had helped run the Glass of Milk program. That's when Moyano knew she had to speak out against the Shining Path. She knew it was dangerous to stand up to the Shining Path. But she did it anyway. On September 27, 1991, she gave a speech. She said the Shining Path should stop killing people. That was all it took. Right away, Moyano became the group's next target.

6   The Shining Path tried to scare Moyano. They bombed buildings where she worked. They blew up food that she had planned to give to the poor. Next they tried to turn people against her. They said Moyano stole money from the programs she ran. They said she was stealing from the people.

7   Then the Shining Path made plans to kill her. They said that if she didn't leave the country, she would soon be dead.

8   Moyano's friends begged her to listen to the Shining Path. They told her to go away for a while. At last, she agreed. She made plans to leave Peru for a few months. But she stayed away just ten days. Moyano could not turn her back on her country. She returned to her role as a leader of the people. She knew the Shining Path was still her enemy. But she said, "This is my life. If they're going to kill me, they're going to kill me."

9   During this time, Moyano wrote a short book about her life called *The Autobiography of Maria Elena Moyano.* In it she said, "There are people who ask if I am afraid. Yes, at times I am, but I am very firm and have moral strength. I have always been ready to surrender my life."

10 In December 1991, the Shining Path struck once more. They attacked a friend of Moyano's. This woman helped run the family kitchens. Members of the Shining Path went to the woman's home. There they shot her. They did not kill her. But they wounded her.

11 Still, Moyano would not give up. On February 14, 1992, she led a march for peace. She did it to remind people that violence is wrong. Her friends feared the march would anger the Shining Path even more. These friends did their best to keep Moyano safe. They did not let her stay in her own home that night. They made sure her bodyguard stayed close to her. But it was not enough. The very next night Moyano went to a public dinner. Shining Path members forced their way into the dinner. They shot and killed Moyano.

12 No one could believe it. At the age of 33, Maria Elena Moyano was dead. Said one man, "It was a death foretold, but it was still a great shock." He said that nobody thought the Shining Path would really do it.

13 Moyano was dead, but she was not forgotten. She would always be a symbol of hope for the people of Peru. One newspaper said that the Shining Path shot Moyano but "they couldn't kill her. She continues to fight for peace."

A Finding the Main Idea

One statement below tells the main idea of the article. One statement is too general, or too broad. The other statement explains only part of the article; it is too narrow. Label the statements using the following key:

M—Main Idea   B—Too Broad   N—Too Narrow

_____ 1. The life and early death of Maria Moyano show how hard it is to make life better for poor people.

_____ 2. Maria Moyano grew up poor. She helped set up programs to help poor families in her country, Peru.

_____ 3. Maria Moyano helped poor people in Peru to work together to make life better. Her enemies killed her.

Score 4 points for each correct answer.

_____ **Total Score:** Finding the Main Idea

B Recalling Facts

How well do you remember the facts in the article? Put an X in the box next to the answer that correctly completes each statement.

1. Maria Moyano first started programs to help others

☐ a. when she was a child.
☐ b. when she was a young mother.
☐ c. when her children started school.

2. The aim of the Glass of Milk program was to give every poor child at least one glass of milk

☐ a. each day.
☐ b. at every meal.
☐ c. with the school lunch.

3. Maria Moyano did not like the Shining Path because

☐ a. its members stole money from programs she ran.
☐ b. its leaders were not from Peru.
☐ c. its leaders used violence to get their way.

4. The day before she died, Moyano

☐ a. came back to Peru after a few months out of the country.
☐ b. led a march for peace.
☐ c. wrote a short book about her life.

Score 4 points for each correct answer.

_____ **Total Score:** Recalling Facts

C | Making Inferences

When you draw a conclusion that is not directly stated in the text, you are making an inference. Put an X in the box next to the statement that is a correct inference.

1.

- ☐ a. Maria Moyano's maid washed rich people's clothes in her home.
- ☐ b. Maria Moyano's mother washed rich people's clothes by hand.
- ☐ c. Maria Moyano's mother charged rich people for making their clothes.

2.

- ☐ a. Maria Moyano's friends thought she might be safe in a public place.
- ☐ b. Maria Moyano was the only famous person in Peru who took a stand against the Shining Path.
- ☐ c. After killing Maria Moyano, the Shining Path stopped causing trouble in Peru.

Score 4 points for each correct answer.

_____ **Total Score:** Making Inferences

D | Using Words

Put an X in the box next to the definition below that is closest in meaning to the underlined word.

1. The <u>violence</u> of the storm made everyone fear that the house would be blown down.

- ☐ a. rough acts that can hurt people or things
- ☐ b. a sudden move that comes as a surprise
- ☐ c. a loud, roaring sound that may last for a long time

2. I believe my cousin will do what is fair because his thinking is <u>moral</u>.

- ☐ a. not likely to take chances
- ☐ b. based on an interest in what is new
- ☐ c. based on what is right and good

3. Which <u>symbol</u> of the United States is used more often, the flag or Uncle Sam?

- ☐ a. sign
- ☐ b. picture
- ☐ c. state

4. The leaders decided to hold a <u>public</u> meeting instead of a private one.

- ☐ a. closed
- ☐ b. open to everyone
- ☐ c. short

5. I don't know how to cook, but I can make a <u>decent</u> sandwich.

   ☐ a. without any taste
   ☐ b. fairly good
   ☐ c. among the worst

6. Our team's <u>struggle</u> to win this ball game ended with my home run!

   ☐ a. the act of trying, over and over, to do something hard
   ☐ b. a group of people working to do something special
   ☐ c. decision to give up

Score 4 points for each correct answer.

_____ **Total Score:** Using Words

E Author's Approach

Put an X in the box next to the correct answer.

1. What is the author's purpose in writing this article?

   ☐ a. to get the reader to give money to the poor
   ☐ b. to tell the reader about a kind and brave woman
   ☐ c. to describe what happens when anyone helps the poor

2. From the statements below, choose the one that you believe the author would agree with.

   ☐ a. When Maria Moyano would not do what they wanted, members of the Shining Path were right to kill her.
   ☐ b. One person cannot make much difference in solving a big problem such as feeding poor people.
   ☐ c. Leaders of the Shining Path were not as brave as Maria Moyano.

3. Choose the statement below that is the weakest argument for writing about Maria Moyano.

   ☐ a. She started programs that made life better for many poor people, especially children.
   ☐ b. She was born poor but became famous.
   ☐ c. She was willing to die to help others.

Score 4 points for each correct answer.

_____ **Total Score:** Author's Approach

F | Summarizing and Paraphrasing

Put an X in the box next to the correct answer.

1. Which summary says all the important things about the article?

☐ a. Maria Moyano led other poor people of Peru to help themselves. When she took a stand for peace and against a group that used violence, members of that group killed her.

☐ b. Maria Moyano was born poor and wanted to make life better for all poor people in Peru. She started many programs. One program provided a glass of milk for each child each day. She died in 1992.

☐ c. Maria Moyano was a famous person in Peru. She said bad things about a group called the Shining Path, so that group killed her.

2. Which sentence means the same thing as the following sentence? "Moyano could not turn her back on her country."

☐ a. Moyano wanted to keep her eyes on what was happening around her.

☐ b. Moyano did not want to stop helping the people who needed her.

☐ c. Moyano did not want to hurt the feelings of anybody around her.

Score 4 points for each correct answer.
_____ **Total Score:** Summarizing and Paraphrasing

G | Critical Thinking

Put an X in the box next to the correct answer.

1. Choose the statement below that states a fact.

☐ a. From 1980 to the present, the Shining Path caused more than 30,000 deaths.

☐ b. Maria Moyano should have left Peru to get away from the Shining Path.

☐ c. If the Shining Path had not killed her friend, Moyano probably would not have paid attention to the group.

2. What was the effect of Maria Moyano's early life?

☐ a. Her mother had trouble finding jobs washing clothes.

☐ b. Her family struggled to survive.

☐ c. She wanted to make life better for poor people.

3. In which paragraph did you find the information to answer question 2?

☐ a. paragraph 1

☐ b. paragraph 2

☐ c. paragraph 9

4. Which lesson about life does this story teach?

☐ a. Never trust anyone.

☐ b. Be true to yourself.

☐ c. Things always turn out well in the end.

5. From the information in the article, you can conclude that

☐ a. the Shining Path has not been punished for Moyano's death.

☐ b. members of the Shining Path have left Peru.

☐ c. Moyano's friends are safe from the Shining Path.

Score 4 points for each correct answer.

_____ **Total Score:** Critical Thinking

Enter your score for each activity. Add the scores together. Record your total score on the graph on page 115.

_____ Finding the Main Idea

_____ Recalling Facts

_____ Making Inferences

_____ Using Words

_____ Author's Approach

_____ Summarizing and Paraphrasing

_____ Critical Thinking

_____ **Total Score**

Personal Response

Would you tell other students to read this article? Explain.

_____

_____

Self-Assessment

While reading the article, _____

_____

was the easiest for me.

A Long, Cold Night

Eleven-year-old Leia Hunt did not see it coming. Her father, David, didn't either. Leia and David were on a snowmobile trip on March 3, 2003. They had made other snowmobile trips in the past. They had never had a problem. For hours they rode along lovely wooded trails in Quebec, Canada. Late in the day, they came to the small town of St. Jerome. Then they took a trail out of town. But this trail held a hidden danger. A drainpipe lay in their way. The pipe was covered with snow, so the Hunts could not see it. When they hit it, they flipped out of control.

2   The snowmobile rolled down a steep bank. It crashed in icy water at the bottom. David smashed his leg in the fall. He could not move. Leia was not hurt. But she was very frightened. And she had a right to be. The two of them were now stuck in this remote spot. The air was cold and getting colder. Night was falling. And the nearest help was miles away, back in St. Jerome. Things looked bad for David and Leia.

Eleven-year-old Leia Hunt and her father, David, play a game in the hospital.

3   David was in terrible pain. Still, he tried to be brave. He asked Leia to gather firewood. She scrambled up the steep bank and looked around. She found some branches from a dead tree and then tried to make her way back down the bank to help her dad. But it was icy. Part way down, she slipped. She tumbled to the bottom of the bank and landed in freezing water up to her knees. Water leaked into her boots. Soon her wet feet were freezing.

4   David and Leia hurried to get a small fire started. But it did not help much. It burned for a while. Then the wind blew it out. Leia and her father sat in the darkness, talking about what to do. They agreed that Leia should try to walk the two miles back to St. Jerome. And so she set out. The temperature was below zero. The wind howled in her ears. Then she heard a different kind of howling—the howling of wolves.

5   Terrified, Leia screamed for her father. "Daddy! Daddy!" she yelled.

6   David heard her shouts. By this time, his body was in terrible pain. He almost could not think straight. But he called out to his daughter to come back to him.

7   Leia came sliding down the steep bank. She curled up next to her father. "Just lie here, baby," David told her. "The groomers will be along any time now to groom the trail, and we'll be fine." Groomers are workers who make sure the trails are clear.

8   But no groomers came by. As the hours slowly passed, David tried to comfort Leia. He urged her not to lose hope. "We're survivors," he said. "They don't bury survivors. And we have faith and we have hope and we'll pull through it."

9   By morning David could not stop shaking. Once again he asked Leia if she would go for help. She was still very scared. But as she later said, "It all happened so fast that I didn't have time to think about it. I wasn't just going to sit there and watch my dad in pain." And so she said she would.

10   It was not easy for her to move. Her feet were frozen. She could not feel them at all. Her boots were covered with ice. David later said, "I had to break ice off her boots before she was finally able to get up and walk on her feet."

11   "Remember," David told her as she headed off, "I'll always be there with you."

12   Somehow Leia climbed up the bank on her frozen feet. Step by step she stumbled down the trail. She was almost too tired and too cold to move. Again and again she wanted to sit down and give up. She forced herself not to do it. She also tried not to think of the wolves. She could see animals down below the trail. They frightened her. "I stopped a couple of times," she later said, "because I was scared." But each time she thought of her father. He was counting on her. And his words still rang in her head. *Remember, I'll always be there with you.* Leia was comforted by those words. They gave her the strength to go on.

13   After three hours Leia came to a store on the edge of town. At about the same time, a group of snowmobilers found David. Quickly, both Leia and David were given help. It turned out that David's knee was broken in seven places. His toes were frozen too. Leia's feet were in even worse shape. It took rescuers 20 minutes to remove the boot on Leia's left foot and another 30 minutes to remove the other boot. The front part of her left foot was frozen. Her right foot was completely frozen. Doctors tried to save it. But they couldn't. They had to cut it off. They also had to cut off the toes of her left foot.

14   David could barely express his pride in Leia. He was amazed that she had walked so far on frozen feet. He praised her courage and bravery. "I don't know how she did it, but I know she did it for me," he said. As he told one reporter, "She's my hero."

A | Finding the Main Idea

One statement below tells the main idea of the article. One statement is too general, or too broad. The other statement explains only part of the article; it is too narrow. Label the statements using the following key:

M—Main Idea   B—Too Broad   N—Too Narrow

_____ 1. Leia and David Hunt were having fun on their snowmobile. But they learned that snowmobiles can be dangerous.

_____ 2. Leia and David Hunt crashed their snowmobile into an icy stream in Quebec, Canada. The crash happened after they hit a hidden drainpipe.

_____ 3. David Hunt was hurt badly in a snowmobile crash in Quebec. His daughter, Leia, bravely walked for hours on frozen feet to get help for her father.

Score 4 points for each correct answer.

_____ **Total Score:** Finding the Main Idea

B | Recalling Facts

How well do you remember the facts in the article? Put an X in the box next to the answer that correctly completes each statement.

1. The Hunts did not see the drainpipe because

☐ a. they were not being careful.
☐ b. it was hidden by snow.
☐ c. David fell asleep while driving.

2. Leia fell into freezing water when she

☐ a. tried to get firewood.
☐ b. tried to walk to St. Jerome the first time.
☐ c. reached the store at the edge of town.

3. The first time Leia went for help, she turned back because of

☐ a. the pain in her frozen feet.
☐ b. a terrible snowstorm.
☐ c. howling wolves.

4. David was rescued by

☐ a. Leia.
☐ b. a group of snowmobilers.
☐ c. a store owner.

Score 4 points for each correct answer.

_____ **Total Score:** Recalling Facts

C | Making Inferences

When you draw a conclusion that is not directly stated in the text, you are making an inference. Put an X in the box next to the statement that is a correct inference.

1.

☐ a. The only time wolves howl is when they are attacking.
☐ b. Wolves never attack girls walking alone.
☐ c. Leia felt safer staying close to David.

2.

☐ a. David and Leia got along well together.
☐ b. David and Leia often fought with each other.
☐ c. David and Leia had ridden over that forest trail many times before.

Score 4 points for each correct answer.

_____ **Total Score:** Making Inferences

D | Using Words

Put an X in the box next to the definition below that is closest in meaning to the underlined word.

1. The hunters went to a <u>remote</u> spot deep in the forest.

☐ a. busy
☐ b. near
☐ c. far away

2. The bike paths in our city park are so nice! Workers must <u>groom</u> them every day.

☐ a. build up
☐ b. make neat
☐ c. break apart

3. He <u>urged</u> me to eat the whole pizza, but I left some for you.

☐ a. feared doing something
☐ b. encouraged to do something
☐ c. stopped

4. Your dog <u>howled</u> all night, and the noise kept me awake.

☐ a. made long, loud cries
☐ b. scratched its ear
☐ c. wagged its tail

5. Some writers <u>express</u> their feelings in songs.

☐ a. read about
☐ b. cover up
☐ c. put into words

6. The children were <u>amazed</u> by her magic trick. Their eyes widened, and their mouths dropped open.

☐ a. cheered up
☐ b. surprised
☐ c. stopped

Score 4 points for each correct answer.

_____ **Total Score:** Using Words

E | **Author's Approach**

Put an X in the box next to the correct answer.

1. The main purpose of the first paragraph is to

☐ a. tell about the courage of Leia Hunt.
☐ b. describe how the Hunts got into trouble.
☐ c. describe the snowmobile trails in Quebec, Canada.

2. From the statements below, choose the one that you believe the author would agree with.

☐ a. David Hunt did not know how to drive a snowmobile very well.
☐ b. It is foolish to feel afraid of wolves.
☐ c. Leia Hunt did all she could to help her father.

3. The author probably wrote this article in order to

☐ a. make people want to go to Quebec on vacation.
☐ b. explain how to drive a snowmobile safely.
☐ c. show how brave Leia Hunt was.

Score 4 points for each correct answer.

_____ **Total Score:** Author's Approach

F | Summarizing and Paraphrasing

Put an X in the box next to the correct answer.

1. Which summary says all the important things about the article?

☐ a. Riding a snowmobile in Canada, David and Leia Hunt had a bad accident. David's leg was smashed. Leia walked two miles on frozen feet to get help. David calls her his hero.

☐ b. David and Leia Hunt crashed their snowmobile. Howling wolves scared Leia when she started to walk to a small town called St. Jerome in Quebec.

☐ c. David Hunt is proud of his daughter, Leia. Their snowmobile went out of control, slid down a hill, and crashed. Both he and Leia were hurt, but they survived. This happened in Canada.

2. Which sentence means the same thing as the following sentence? "David almost could not express his pride in Leia."

☐ a. David could not believe that he was proud of Leia.

☐ b. David had trouble putting into words how proud he was of Leia.

☐ c. David could not say he was proud of Leia.

Score 4 points for each correct answer.

_____ **Total Score:** Summarizing and Paraphrasing

G | Critical Thinking

Put an X in the box next to the correct answer.

1. Choose the statement below that states an opinion.

☐ a. David tried to stay calm after the crash.

☐ b. No one else could have been as brave as Leia.

☐ c. Leia's right foot got so cold that it completely froze.

2. From information in the article, you can predict that

☐ a. the Hunts will remember this trip for the rest of their lives.

☐ b. David will never again count on Leia when he is in trouble.

☐ c. people will not be allowed to drive snowmobiles on snowy trails in Canada ever again.

3. David and Leia are alike because

☐ a. each one smashed a leg.

☐ b. they froze their feet and each one lost one foot.

☐ c. neither one saw the hidden pipe.

4. Leia was afraid on her long walk back to St. Jerome. What was one cause of her fear?

☐ a. She was afraid of the wolves.

☐ b. She was afraid that she was lost.

☐ c. She was afraid of the dark.

5. In which paragraphs did you find the information to answer question 4?

☐ a. paragraphs 1, 2, and 3

☐ b. paragraphs 3, 9, and 11

☐ c. paragraphs 4, 5, and 12

Score 4 points for each correct answer.

_____ **Total Score:** Critical Thinking

Enter your score for each activity. Add the scores together. Record your total score on the graph on page 115.

_____ Finding the Main Idea

_____ Recalling Facts

_____ Making Inferences

_____ Using Words

_____ Author's Approach

_____ Summarizing and Paraphrasing

_____ Critical Thinking

_____ **Total Score**

Personal Response

A question I would like Leia to answer is "_____

_____

_____?"

Self-Assessment

I can't really understand how _____

_____

_____

Trapped in a Canyon

Aron Ralston is shown here climbing in the Rocky Mountains in March 2003.

Aron Ralston did not plan to spend the night in Bluejohn Canyon. He thought he would be back at his truck by the end of day. The 27-year-old Ralston was an expert rock climber. He thought he could make the 15-mile trip with no problem. On Saturday, April 26, 2003, Ralston set out. At first he made his way quickly. He liked hiking through this wild and rocky part of Utah. The trip started out well, but it soon took a bad turn. Within hours Aron Ralston was trapped.

2   The trouble came at 2:45 P.M. Ralston was hiking in a canyon. A canyon is a narrow valley between two cliffs. He was trying to squeeze through a tight spot. As he moved past a huge rock, it suddenly moved. Ralston tried to get out of the way. But he could not. The 800-pound rock rolled against his right hand. It pinned the hand—and Ralston—to the canyon wall.

3   Ralston felt panic rise in his chest. He threw himself at the rock, trying to push it off his hand. It was no use. At last he calmed down and began to think about his options. His first hope was that someone would come by to help him. That was not likely. Few climbers came through this canyon. It could be days or even weeks before the next person came through.

4   Ralston thought he might be able to break up the rock. He had a small knife in his pocket. Perhaps he could chip away enough of the rock to get his hand out. But the rock was too hard, and Ralston's knife was no help. He could not break off any chunks of the rock.

5   Next Ralston thought about his climbing tools. He wondered if he could use any of them to push or pull the rock away. But he had nothing in his bag that would work. No matter how hard he tried, he could not get the rock to budge.

6   Ralston could think of only one other way to escape. It was almost too grim to consider. Still, in the back of his mind, the shocking thought was there: He could cut off his own hand.

7   He was not that desperate, at least not yet. So he settled down and waited. As the hours passed, he listened for sounds of other hikers. No one came. All through the night Ralston waited. The next day passed, and the next. Ralston had a little food and water with him. He tried to make it last. He took small bites of his burritos and tiny sips of water. Still, by Tuesday morning, his food and water were gone.

8   At that point Ralston decided to act. He would try to cut off his hand to save his life. He pulled out his knife. Then he took a deep breath and pushed the knife against his right wrist.

9   "I started sawing back and forth," he later said, "and didn't even break the skin. I couldn't even cut the hair off my arm, the knife was so dull."

10 It was no use. Ralston could not do it. He put the knife down. Again, he settled back to wait for help. But with no more food or water, he grew weaker and weaker. By Thursday morning he was running out of time. Soon, he knew, it would be too late. He would die here in this lonely canyon.

11 That thought made Ralston truly desperate. He decided to try, once more, to cut off his hand.

12 First he had to build up his courage. He took his knife and carved himself a message in the rock. "Good Luck," he spelled out. Then he carved out one more word: "Now."

13 Ralston knew the knife was not sharp enough to cut through bone. So before he started cutting, he had to snap the two bones in his wrist. For five minutes, he pushed and twisted with all his might. At last, he felt one of the bones snap. After a few more minutes, the second bone broke.

14 Next Ralston picked up the knife. He ignored the pain that shot through his arm. He forced himself to cut deeper and deeper into his skin. Blood dripped onto the rock. Still, he kept at it. Later Ralston said, "I did what I had to do."

15 That was true, but it took amazing courage. "I don't know if I could have done it," said one climber. "I'd probably just die."

16 Even after Ralston cut off his hand, he was not out of danger. He had to get out of the canyon while he still had the strength. He tied a strip of cloth tightly around his right arm. That slowed the bleeding. Then he began the long trek out. At one point he came to a cliff. It was 60 feet to the bottom. With his good arm, he got out a rope. Somehow he lowered himself down that cliff.

17 Near the end of the trail, Ralston met two climbers. They stayed with him until a rescue helicopter came. At last Aron Ralston was safe. And although he was now missing a hand, most people thought he would soon be out climbing again. "Cutting off his hand will stop him for a month, and that's about it," said one climber. "What a dude."

A | Finding the Main Idea

One statement below tells the main idea of the article. One statement is too general, or too broad. The other statement explains only part of the article; it is too narrow. Label the statements using the following key:

M—Main Idea   B—Too Broad   N—Too Narrow

_____ 1. Not many people would be brave enough to do what climber Aron Ralston did. His climbing accident made him do what he had to do to stay alive.

_____ 2. Climber Aron Ralston got stuck in a canyon when a huge rock rolled on top of his hand. To save his life, he cut off his hand. Then he climbed out to safety.

_____ 3. Climber Aron Ralston waited for help from Saturday until Thursday. By Tuesday his food and water were gone. So he decided to cut off his own hand with a small, dull knife.

Score 4 points for each correct answer.

_____ **Total Score:** Finding the Main Idea

B | Recalling Facts

How well do you remember the facts in the article? Put an X in the box next to the answer that correctly completes each statement.

1. Aron Ralston became trapped

☐ a. in the early morning.
☐ b. in the middle of the afternoon.
☐ c. just as the sun was going down.

2. Ralston couldn't break the big rock because

☐ a. the rock was too hard.
☐ b. he was too weak from losing a lot of blood.
☐ c. he couldn't reach the rock with his left hand.

3. Just before Ralston cut off his hand, he

☐ a. took a long drink of water.
☐ b. broke his wrist bones.
☐ c. wrote a letter to his mother.

4. Ralston was taken to safety

☐ a. in a helicopter.
☐ b. after passing out.
☐ c. in a fire truck.

Score 4 points for each correct answer.

_____ **Total Score:** Recalling Facts

C | Making Inferences

When you draw a conclusion that is not directly stated in the text, you are making an inference. Put an X in the box next to the statement that is a correct inference.

1.

☐ a. If Ralston had waited just a few more days, he would have been saved by hikers.

☐ b. Ralston probably would not have needed to cut off his hand if he had hiked with a friend.

☐ c. Ralston couldn't think straight after being stuck for three days.

2.

☐ a. This was the first time Ralston had hiked alone.

☐ b. Ralston should not have waited so long to cut off his hand.

☐ c. Ralston was in a lot of pain.

Score 4 points for each correct answer.

_____ **Total Score:** Making Inferences

D | Using Words

Put an X in the box next to the definition below that is closest in meaning to the underlined word.

1. A heavy box fell on her foot and <u>pinned</u> it to the floor so she could not move.

☐ a. surprised
☐ b. held in place
☐ c. bent

2. <u>Panic</u> went through the crowd when someone shouted, "Fire!"

☐ a. a wind
☐ b. noise
☐ c. fear

3. He read all the <u>options</u> on the menu and then ordered a bowl of soup.

☐ a. choices
☐ b. words
☐ c. answers

4. She looked <u>grim</u> as she gave us the bad news.

☐ a. tired
☐ b. interested
☐ c. serious

5. Will you at least <u>consider</u> coming with us?

☐ a. think about
☐ b. ask someone about
☐ c. tell us about

6. Hunger made the men so <u>desperate</u> that they ate leaves and grass to stay alive.

☐ a. silly
☐ b. tired and sleepy
☐ c. crazy with worry

Score 4 points for each correct answer.

_____ **Total Score:** Using Words

E | Author's Approach

Put an X in the box next to the correct answer.

1. What is the author's purpose in writing this article?

☐ a. to get the reader to take up hiking
☐ b. to show how rescue teams work
☐ c. to tell what happened when one brave person faced a hard problem

2. Choose the statement below that best describes the author's opinion in paragraph 15.

☐ a. The author thinks that Ralston is foolish.
☐ b. The author thinks that Ralston is brave.
☐ c. The author thinks that Ralston is clever.

3. The author tells this story mainly by

☐ a. describing story events in the order they happened.
☐ b. comparing different topics or different ideas.
☐ c. using his or her imagination.

Score 4 points for each correct answer.

_____ **Total Score:** Author's Approach

F | Summarizing and Paraphrasing

Put an X in the box next to the correct answer.

1. Which summary says all the important things about the article?

☐ a. Aron Ralston had to cut off his hand on a hiking trip. He slowed the bleeding with a tight bandage around his arm. Ralston showed great courage.

☐ b. A huge rock fell on climber Aron Ralston's hand. Stuck in a canyon for days, Ralston finally got free by cutting off his hand. He climbed out and survived.

☐ c. Aron Ralston showed great courage after a terrible accident. He broke the wrist bones of his right hand. He cut off the hand too.

2. Which sentence means the same thing as the following sentence? "And although he was now missing a hand, most people thought he would soon be out climbing again."

☐ a. Now most people think he is missing a hand.

☐ b. Most people think that he will soon climb again, even though he now has only one hand.

☐ c. Most people who are missing a hand are soon out climbing again.

Score 4 points for each correct answer.

_____ **Total Score:** Summarizing and Paraphrasing

G | Critical Thinking

Put an X in the box next to the correct answer.

1. Choose the statement below that states an opinion.

☐ a. Bluejohn Canyon is in Utah.
☐ b. Ralston carried a knife with him on the hike.
☐ c. Ralston should have waited for help a few days longer.

2. What caused Ralston to decide to eat his food and water slowly?

☐ a. Ralston wanted the food and water to last.
☐ b. Ralston didn't like the taste of the food and water.
☐ c. Ralston wanted to share his food and water with the person who would rescue him.

3. In which paragraph did you find the information to answer question 2?

☐ a. paragraph 7
☐ b. paragraph 9
☐ c. paragraph 13

4. Which lesson about life does this story teach?

☐ a. Waiting for help makes more sense than helping yourself.
☐ b. People can do amazing things when they must.
☐ c. Nature is always kind to us.

5. How could you use the information in the article to increase your chances of staying safe while hiking?

☐ a. I would always hike in a rocky place.

☐ b. I would remember to take enough food and water to last at least a month.

☐ c. I would always hike with a partner.

Score 4 points for each correct answer.

_____ **Total Score:** Critical Thinking

Enter your score for each activity. Add the scores together. Record your total score on the graph on page 115.

_____ Finding the Main Idea

_____ Recalling Facts

_____ Making Inferences

_____ Using Words

_____ Author's Approach

_____ Summarizing and Paraphrasing

_____ Critical Thinking

_____ **Total Score**

Personal Response

I can't believe _____

_____

_____

Self-Assessment

When reading the article, I was having trouble with

_____

_____

_____

LESSON 4

A Young Man Speaks Out

AIDS activist Nkosi Johnson speaks at the 13th International AIDS Conference in Durban, South Africa, in 2000.

Gail Johnson saw it right away. The little boy was sick, very sick. And his mother was dying. Both of them had AIDS. The mother had passed the disease to her son when he was born in 1989. Now the boy, named Nkosi, was two years old. He and his mother had come to an AIDS care center in Johannesburg, South Africa, to seek help.

2   Johnson worked at the center. She had seen an AIDS death in her own family. So she knew what it was like. Her heart went out to little Nkosi. She knew that she wanted to do something more than just talk about AIDS. "And there was Nkosi," Johnson said. "All I had to do was to reach out to him."

3   Nkosi's mother had left her hometown to seek help. But she had left for a second reason as well. She feared the people in her town. They didn't know that she and Nkosi had AIDS. What would they do if they found out? At that time, AIDS scared many people. Folks feared they could catch it by shaking hands with someone with AIDS or breathing the same air. That was not true, of course. It is not that easy to get AIDS. But many AIDS patients were shunned by their community anyway. Many people would have nothing to do with them. So Nkosi and his mother left before there was trouble.

4   Now Nkosi's mother was too sick to care for him. Johnson offered help. She asked if she could raise Nkosi. His mother agreed. Johnson became his foster mother. The boy took the name Nkosi Johnson.

5   But Nkosi's problems were far from over. In 1997 his mother died. That same year Gail Johnson tried to put Nkosi in a local school. Many parents became angry. They didn't want a child with AIDS in their school. They feared Nkosi would give AIDS to their children. But Gail and Nkosi fought back. Their struggle became a big news story. In the end Gail and Nkosi won. The school accepted Nkosi.

6   Now everyone knew that Nkosi had AIDS. Still, he tried to live a normal life. He loved puzzles. He enjoyed playing cards. But he also spoke out about AIDS. It took a lot of courage. Most adults didn't want to talk about it. But here was a little boy leading the way. People began to listen. They wanted to hear what he had to say. "Nkosi made a lot of adults think," his doctor said. He added that Nkosi was very brave.

7   In his own way, Nkosi was living up to his name. In the Zulu language, *nkosi* means "king of kings."

8   In 2000 Nkosi gave the best speech of his life. Over 10,000 people gathered to hear him. By now Nkosi was

11 years old. But AIDS had made him very sick. As he walked onto the stage, a bright spotlight shined on him. He looked frail. His shiny black suit hung on his body. He was thin. His belt had six extra holes punched in it. He looked so weak that people feared he might drop the microphone. He didn't.

9   Nkosi looked out at the crowd. Then he took a deep breath. He began by telling his story. "Hi," he said, "my name is Nkosi Johnson. . . . and I have full-blown AIDS." He told the people what it was like to have AIDS. "I hate having AIDS because I get very sick," he said. "I get very sad when I think of all the other children and babies that are sick with AIDS."

10   Nkosi ended by saying, "Care for us and accept us. We are all human beings. We are normal. We have hands. We have feet. We can walk, we can talk, we have needs just like everyone else. Don't be afraid of us—we are all the same." Many people in the audience wiped tears from their eyes.

11   Later that year Nkosi came to the United States. Again he spoke out about AIDS. "It is sad to see so many sick people," he said. "I wish everybody in the world could be well." He continued to teach people.

"You cannot get AIDS by hugging," he reminded them. "You cannot get AIDS by kissing."

12   By now, though, Nkosi was sicker than ever. Soon after he got home, he collapsed. AIDS had reached his brain. Nkosi fought on. But his life was slipping away. At last he went into a coma. He was fed through a tube. People met every day outside his home to pray. But he did not improve. On June 1, 2001, Nkosi died. He was 12 years old. "His race was run," said Gail Johnson. "I think we knew that a long time ago."

13   Thousands of people lined up for Nkosi's funeral. Kenneth Kaunda, a leader in the fight against AIDS, called Nkosi brave. "He has done a great thing. His message helped to break the silence against AIDS."

14   South African leader Nelson Mandela agreed. He said, "It is a great pity that this young man has died. He was very bold." Mandela added that Nkosi had earned the right to be given all honor and respect.

15   Nkosi Johnson had died too young. But he had honored his name. He was indeed brave, a "king of kings."

A | Finding the Main Idea

One statement below tells the main idea of the article. One statement is too general, or too broad. The other statement explains only part of the article; it is too narrow. Label the statements using the following key:

M—Main Idea   B—Too Broad   N—Too Narrow

_____ 1. AIDS is a terrible disease that can kill you, no matter what your age is.

_____ 2. Nkosi's mother came to Johannesburg, South Africa, for help. She had AIDS. So did her son, Nkosi. She died when Nkosi was only eight. Gail Johnson became Nkosi's foster mother.

_____ 3. Young Nkosi had a terrible disease, AIDS. Even so, he gave speeches and taught people about the disease. He died of AIDS at the age of 12.

Score 4 points for each correct answer.

_____ **Total Score:** Finding the Main Idea

B | Recalling Facts

How well do you remember the facts in the article? Put an X in the box next to the answer that correctly completes each statement.

1. Nkosi got AIDS

☐ a. from his mother.
☐ b. from a kiss.
☐ c. by breathing the same air a person with AIDS breathed.

2. Many parents didn't want Nkosi in their school because

☐ a. their school was too crowded already.
☐ b. he gave too many speeches.
☐ c. they thought he would give AIDS to their children.

3. In his speeches, Nkosi asked people to

☐ a. care for people with AIDS.
☐ b. let him go to school with their children.
☐ c. give him money so he could fight AIDS.

4. Nkosi finally died when AIDS reached his

☐ a. stomach.
☐ b. brain.
☐ c. heart.

Score 4 points for each correct answer.

_____ **Total Score:** Recalling Facts

C Making Inferences

When you draw a conclusion that is not directly stated in the text, you are making an inference. Put an X in the box next to the statement that is a correct inference.

1.

☐ a. People in Nkosi's hometown had never heard of AIDS before he got it.

☐ b. Many people felt sad after hearing Nkosi's speeches.

☐ c. Gail Johnson was foster mother to many children with AIDS.

2.

☐ a. Hardly anyone wanted to hear Nkosi speak when he came to the United States.

☐ b. Gail Johnson talked Nkosi into making speeches about AIDS.

☐ c. AIDS makes people lose weight.

Score 4 points for each correct answer.

_____ **Total Score:** Making Inferences

D Using Words

Put an X in the box next to the definition below that is closest in meaning to the underlined word.

1. This <u>disease</u> makes your body weak.

☐ a. sound

☐ b. problem

☐ c. sickness

2. No one likes to be <u>shunned</u>. It's lonely when no one talks to you or wants to be your friend.

☐ a. helped

☐ b. left alone

☐ c. forgotten

3. My cat is bigger than a <u>normal</u> cat.

☐ a. friendly and happy

☐ b. like nothing else in the world

☐ c. like others in its group

4. The doorman carried the heavy box for the <u>frail</u> old man.

☐ a. weak

☐ b. nice

☐ c. sad

5. When Nkosi went into a <u>coma</u>, doctors had to feed him through a tube.

- ☐ a. a sad state
- ☐ b. a state much like deep sleep
- ☐ c. a state of great excitement

6. To fight a giant, a knight had to be <u>bold</u>.

- ☐ a. brave
- ☐ b. kind
- ☐ c. shy

Score 4 points for each correct answer.

_____ **Total Score:** Using Words

E | **Author's Approach**

Put an X in the box next to the correct answer.

1. The main purpose of the first paragraph is to

- ☐ a. tell why Gail Johnson liked Nkosi.
- ☐ b. explain that Nkosi and his mother had AIDS.
- ☐ c. describe the AIDS disease.

2. From the statements below, choose the one that you believe the author would agree with.

- ☐ a. Nkosi helped all people with AIDS.
- ☐ b. Nkosi was afraid of other people with AIDS.
- ☐ c. Nkosi complained a lot about his problems.

3. The author probably wrote this article in order to

- ☐ a. make readers feel sorry for Nkosi.
- ☐ b. show readers how brave Nkosi was.
- ☐ c. describe how badly Nkosi was treated.

Score 4 points for each correct answer.

_____ **Total Score:** Author's Approach

F Summarizing and Paraphrasing

Put an X in the box next to the correct answer.

1. Which summary says all the important things about the article?

☐ a. Nkosi Johnson, who got AIDS from his mother, told others about the disease. He was born in Africa. He visited the United States in 2000.

☐ b. Nkosi Johnson wanted others to accept those with AIDS. Born in Africa, Nkosi made speeches about AIDS to people in Africa and in the United States.

☐ c. Nkosi Johnson, a young man with AIDS, taught people about the disease. He reminded people that those with AIDS are people too. Many were sad when he died of AIDS at the age of 12.

2. Which sentence means the same thing as the following sentence? "She had seen an AIDS death in her own family."

☐ a. AIDS had disappeared in her family.
☐ b. One of her family members had died of AIDS.
☐ c. Her whole family had died of AIDS.

Score 4 points for each correct answer.

_____ **Total Score:** Summarizing and Paraphrasing

G Critical Thinking

Put an X in the box next to the correct answer.

1. Choose the statement below that states a fact.

☐ a. More money should be spent to find a cure for AIDS.
☐ b. AIDS is the worst disease ever.
☐ c. More than 10,000 people heard Nkosi speak one day.

2. Kenneth Kaunda and Nelson Mandela are alike because

☐ a. they both were with Nkosi when he died.
☐ b. they both had AIDS.
☐ c. they both were proud of Nkosi.

3. Nkosi and his mother left their hometown. What was one cause of that action?

☐ a. They wanted to see more of the world before they died of AIDS.

☐ b. They were afraid of how the town would treat them because they had AIDS.

☐ c. They had heard of Gail Johnson and wanted to meet her before they died.

4. In which paragraph did you find the information to answer question 3?

☐ a. paragraph 2
☐ b. paragraph 3
☐ c. paragraph 4

5. How is Nkosi Johnson an example of uncommon courage?

☐ a. He told people what they needed to know but didn't want to hear.

☐ b. He died of AIDS at a very young age.

☐ c. He and his mother left their hometown before there was trouble.

Score 4 points for each correct answer.

_____ **Total Score:** Critical Thinking

Enter your score for each activity. Add the scores together. Record your total score on the graph on page 115.

_____ Finding the Main Idea

_____ Recalling Facts

_____ Making Inferences

_____ Using Words

_____ Author's Approach

_____ Summarizing and Paraphrasing

_____ Critical Thinking

_____ **Total Score**

Personal Response

Would you tell other students to read this article? Explain.

_____

_____

Self-Assessment

A word or phrase in the article that I do not understand is

_____

_____

Compare and Contrast

Pick two stories in Unit One. Tell about someone who put himself or herself in danger.
Use information from the stories to fill in this chart.

Title	What danger did this person face?	Whom did this person help?	How did this person show courage?

Imagine you were one of these brave people. Write an entry in your diary. _____

_____

_____

UNIT TWO

In the Line of Fire

One day Alfred Rascon saw some soldiers near his California home. They were practicing jumping out of planes with parachutes. The seven-year-old boy wanted to be like them. So he made his own parachute out of a sheet. He climbed onto the roof of his house and jumped. Of course, his "chute" didn't work. The fall broke his wrist. But it did not kill his spirit.

2   Rascon was born in Mexico. When he was a young boy, his family moved to the United States. His parents worked on farms near Los Angeles. Although Rascon was not a citizen, he fell in love with his new country.

3   He had no money for college. So after high school Rascon hoped to join the Army. He was only 17 years old. That meant he needed his parents' permission. He begged them to let him go. At last they said yes. Rascon was later asked why he was so eager to fight for the United States. After all, he was still not a citizen. "I was always an American in my heart," he answered.

4   In the Army Rascon became a medic. A medic is not a doctor. But in war, he or she is often the closest thing there is. A medic treats wounded soldiers. He or she tries to keep them alive until they get to a hospital.

5   By the time he was 20 years old, Rascon was in the war in Vietnam. On March 16, 1966, he was in the jungle with his unit. Suddenly the enemy opened fire. Bullets ripped through the air. Grenades burst all around. One soldier said it was "ten minutes of pure hell. It looked like it was snowing fire."

6   A man with a machine gun was hit first. He cried out, "Medic! Medic!"

7   But Rascon was told to stay where he was. It was too dangerous to go to the wounded man just yet. Rascon was supposed to wait until his unit could fight back. That way Rascon would be protected. But Rascon knew the man needed help right away. So he didn't wait. Instead, he dashed through the storm of enemy bullets. He managed to reach the wounded gunner. Then Rascon placed his body between the man and the enemy fire. Soon a bullet hit Rascon in the hip. It went through his body and out his shoulder blade.

8   Despite his wounds, Rascon dragged the gunner out of danger. Sadly, the man soon died. Rascon then remembered the machine gun. It was still out where the gunner had fallen. Fearing the enemy might grab it, Rascon crawled back to get it. As he made his way along, a grenade exploded right next to him. Pieces of

---

Alfred Rascon receives the Medal of Honor from President Clinton in Washington, D.C., in 2000.

metal flew into his stomach and face. "Oh my god," he thought for a moment, "my face is gone."

9   At last Rascon reached the machine gun. He dragged it back to his unit. Saving the gun saved lives. One soldier said that without the gun the front of the unit would have been attacked by the enemy.

10   Rascon was not done yet. He saw another soldier who had been shot. Worse, Rascon saw a grenade land right near this man. Rascon threw himself on the wounded man just before the grenade blew up. In doing so, Rascon saved the man's life. But he himself suffered more wounds. By now he bled from his ears and nose. He had also lost his hearing. Yet he found the strength to do it all again. He dove on another man to protect him from another grenade.

11   At last, the enemy backed off. Even then Rascon didn't think of himself. He went on treating wounded men. "I had to take care of my friends," he said later. "That's what it was all about. And it wasn't a question of being afraid because I already was afraid."

12   Men from his unit finally forced Rascon to stop working. They put him on a helicopter. They sent him off to an Army hospital. By this time, Rascon was nearly dead. A chaplain gave him last rites, that is, the special prayers for the dying. But Rascon did not die. In time his wounds healed. The next year Rascon became a citizen of the United States.

13   After the battle, the men in Rascon's unit entered his name to win the Medal of Honor. This is the highest honor the U.S. government gives to a soldier. But for some reason Rascon did not win it. Many years later his old Army friends learned of this. They were outraged. They had always believed he had won that medal. They got the Army to hear Rascon's case again. The Army agreed with the men. In 2000, Alfred Rascon was given the Medal of Honor.

14   At a special program, President Bill Clinton gave Rascon his medal. Clinton also had good words for him. "Thank you for looking out for people when no one else could be there for them," he said. "You have taught us once again that being American has nothing to do with place of birth."

15   Neil Haffy was there to see Rascon get his medal. Haffy was one of the men Rascon had saved. With tears in his eyes, Haffy said, "I have a beautiful wife. I have four children and four grandchildren. I wouldn't have any of that without him. I was dead."

A | Finding the Main Idea

One statement below tells the main idea of the article. One statement is too general, or too broad. The other statement explains only part of the article; it is too narrow. Label the statements using the following key:

M—Main Idea   **B—Too Broad**   **N—Too Narrow**

_____ 1. Although not a U.S. citizen, Alfred Rascon joined the Army. He was in Vietnam in 1966 as a medic. He risked his life over and over to save others and was badly wounded. Later he became a U.S. citizen. He received the Medal of Honor in 2000.

_____ 2. From the time he was a child, Alfred Rascon wanted to do exciting things. His chance came when he was serving in the U.S. Army during the Vietnam War. In 2000 he received the Medal of Honor for his actions at that time.

_____ 3. Alfred Rascon was 17 years old when he joined the U.S. Army. Three years later, when he was in Vietnam as a medic, a soldier with a machine gun called for help. Rascon ran to the gunner and tried to save his life, but the man died.

Score 4 points for each correct answer.

_____ **Total Score:** Finding the Main Idea

B | Recalling Facts

How well do you remember the facts in the article? Put an X in the box next to the answer that correctly completes each statement.

1. In 1966, Alfred Rascon was

☐ a. seven years old.
☐ b. 17 years old.
☐ c. 20 years old.

2. When a soldier firing a machine gun was wounded, Rascon

☐ a. was wounded helping the man.
☐ b. took over the machine gun himself.
☐ c. first dragged the gun to safety.

3. When a grenade landed near a wounded man, Rascon

☐ a. ran for cover.
☐ b. threw himself on the grenade.
☐ c. threw himself on the wounded man.

4. Rascon received the Medal of Honor

☐ a. when he was sent home because of his wounds.
☐ b. at the end of the war in Vietnam.
☐ c. from President Clinton.

Score 4 points for each correct answer.

_____ **Total Score:** Recalling Facts

C | Making Inferences

When you draw a conclusion that is not directly stated in the text, you are making an inference. Put an X in the box next to the statement that is a correct inference.

1.

☐ a. Except for Alfred Rascon, nobody who fought in the Vietnam War won the Medal of Honor.

☐ b. Most soldiers who won the Medal of Honor for actions in Vietnam War received it before 2000.

☐ c. Only soldiers who are U.S. citizens from birth may receive the Medal of Honor.

2.

☐ a. If Rascon's friends had not argued with the Army, he would not have received the Medal of Honor.

☐ b. Rascon and the other men in his unit stayed close after the war, talking to each other at least weekly.

☐ c. Rascon became a citizen only so he could have a better chance of winning a medal.

Score 4 points for each correct answer.

_____ **Total Score:** Making Inferences

D | Using Words

Put an X in the box next to the definition below that is closest in meaning to the underlined word.

1. The soldier jumped from the plane and pulled a cord. His <u>parachute</u> flapped open, filled with air, and carried him gently to the earth.

☐ a. a short, simple story about an everyday event which teaches a lesson

☐ b. a large cloth that is carried folded up but opens like an umbrella to slow the fall of a person or thing dropping from an airplane

☐ c. a very light machine with wings but no engine that glides through the air, usually holding no more than one person

2. Someone born outside the United States may become a <u>citizen</u> of this country after passing a special test.

☐ a. a member of a nation who has full rights, such as the right to vote

☐ b. a person who takes part in a particular action, such as teaching, for pay

☐ c. a person who asks others to vote for him or her for a city, state, or national office, such as president

3. My brother's <u>unit</u> finishes its training next week.

☐ a. a number

☐ b. all the soldiers in an army

☐ c. a group of soldiers who train and work together

4. A <u>grenade</u> landed near a tree. In the blast a moment later, branches flew away from the torn-up stump.

☐ a. a small bomb thrown by hand or fired from a gun
☐ b. a small helicopter that is used for rescues
☐ c. a small tank that holds one person

5. Their <u>chaplain</u> led the soldiers in a short prayer.

☐ a. a singer
☐ b. a doctor
☐ c. a minister

6. The customer was so <u>outraged</u> by the poor service at the store that she demanded to see the manager.

☐ a. left behind
☐ b. angered
☐ c. puzzled

Score 4 points for each correct answer.

_____ **Total Score:** Using Words

E | Author's Approach

Put an X in the box next to the correct answer.

1. The author uses the first sentence of the article to

☐ a. name the main person in the story.
☐ b. describe the qualities of California homes.
☐ c. compare soldiers to other people.

2. Choose the statement below that best describes the author's opinion in paragraph 10.

☐ a. Rascon did what any well-trained soldier would do.
☐ b. Rascon showed extraordinary concern for his fellow soldiers.
☐ c. Rascon was foolish to put himself in danger so often, especially after he was wounded.

3. The author tells this story mainly by

☐ a. asking and answering questions.
☐ b. retelling Rascon's experiences.
☐ c. using his or her own imagination.

Score 4 points for each correct answer.

_____ **Total Score:** Author's Approach

F | Summarizing and Paraphrasing

Put an X in the box next to the correct answer.

1. Which summary says all the important things about the article?

☐ a. During a battle in Vietnam in 1966, Alfred Rascon was wounded while helping a fallen gunner. Then he was wounded again when a grenade exploded nearby.

☐ b. Alfred Rascon, a young Army medic serving in Vietnam in 1966, was badly wounded while saving other men. In 2000 he received the Medal of Honor.

☐ c. After Alfred Rascon was wounded, men in his unit put his name in to win the Medal of Honor. Over 30 years later, they found out he had not received it. They asked for it again, and this time Rascon received it.

2. Which sentence means the same thing as the following sentence? "He dashed through the storm of enemy bullets."

☐ a. Raindrops were falling on enemy bullets when the man ran through the storm.

☐ b. The enemy bullets were making so much noise that the runner thought the noise was thunder.

☐ c. The man ran through very heavy enemy gunfire.

Score 4 points for each correct answer.

_____ **Total Score:** Summarizing and Paraphrasing

G | Critical Thinking

Put an X in the box next to the correct answer.

1. Choose the statement below that states a fact.

☐ a. The Army was wrong not to award the Medal of Honor to Rascon the first time his friends entered his name for the award.

☐ b. Men from Rascon's unit were angry when they learned he had not received the Medal of Honor.

☐ c. Rascon should have argued with the Army himself when he did not receive the Medal of Honor.

2. From information in the article, you can predict that

☐ a. the Army will award the Medal of Honor to any soldier whose friends ask for it for him or her.

☐ b. now that the Medal of Honor matter is settled, Rascon and his Army friends will forget about each other.

☐ c. even after receiving the Medal of Honor, Rascon will not think of his actions as anything unusual.

3. Rascon and his friends in his unit are alike because

☐ a. they both showed real concern for each other.

☐ b. they all received Medals of Honor.

☐ c. none of them were citizens of the U.S. during the time they served in the Army.

4. Rascon dragged a machine gun left by a dying gunner back to his own unit. What was the cause of this action?

☐ a. His unit didn't have enough guns to keep fighting.

☐ b. He knew the enemy would use the gun against his unit.

☐ c. Rascon wanted to use the gun himself.

5. In which paragraphs did you find information to answer question 4?

☐ a. paragraphs 6 and 7

☐ b. paragraphs 8 and 9

☐ c. paragraphs 15 and 16

Score 4 points for each correct answer.

_____ **Total Score:** Critical Thinking

Enter your score for each activity. Add the scores together. Record your total score on the graph on page 115.

_____ Finding the Main Idea

_____ Recalling Facts

_____ Making Inferences

_____ Using Words

_____ Author's Approach

_____ Summarizing and Paraphrasing

_____ Critical Thinking

_____ **Total Score**

Personal Response

I know the feeling _____

_____

_____

Self-Assessment

One of the things I did best when reading this article was

_____

I believe I did this well because _____

_____

Without a Second Thought

Daniel Santos didn't know Maria Cappozza. He had never seen her before. But that didn't matter to 21-year-old Santos. He saw that she was in trouble. And so he acted. He did not wait. As he put it, "I just jumped and did what I had to do."

2 It happened on September 9, 1996. Santos was driving north of New York City. At 4:40 P.M. he was heading over the Tappan Zee Bridge in his pickup truck. Suddenly a driver up in front of him swerved. She drove right into the guardrail. The young woman got out of her car. Then she climbed over the railing.

3 People around her watched in horror. They could not believe what they were seeing. The woman was going to jump. "No, no, no!" they screamed.

4 But Maria Cappozza did not listen. At that moment, she was not thinking clearly. She had given up. She could not see all the good things in life. She had decided to end her life by jumping off the bridge. Without pausing, she threw herself into the Hudson

The Tappan Zee Bridge crosses the Hudson River between South Nyack and Tarrytown, New York.

River 130 feet below. When she hit the water she stopped moving. She just lay face down in the water.

5 The people who saw her jump were shocked. Daniel Santos was as upset as everyone else. But while others just stared, Santos chose to act.

6 "I thought . . . she's going to drown. I've got to do something," he later said.

7 Santos began to take off his shoes. He yelled for people to call 911. He handed his wallet to someone so it would not get wet. And then he climbed over the railing just as Cappozza had done.

8 No one could believe it. Santos was going to try to rescue the woman! He was going to jump 130 feet into the river after her! A jump that far would frighten anyone—and for good reason. It is a very dangerous thing to do. "Water is like stone in a leap from that level," said one New York doctor. He went on to say that most people who have jumped from the Tappan Zee didn't live to tell about it.

9 Santos was not an expert diver. He was a mechanic. He was not trained to do high dives. In fact, he had never done a high dive. He had made a 12-foot dive once. That was it. But as his sister said, "He has a good heart." And so Santos did not think about his own safety. He thought only of the 24-year-old woman who lay in the river below him. He realized that she needed his help.

10 "I admit it was crazy," he later said. "But when you see somebody lying face down in the water like that, and you're afraid they're going to drown, you're going to do something to help them."

11 That's what Santos did. "I just prayed and closed my eyes, and I didn't even think about the bad things that could happen to me," he said.

12 Before people could stop him, he jumped.

13 When he hit the water, the force nearly knocked him out. "It felt like I got hit by a truck," he said. He broke a rib. One of his lungs collapsed. And every part of his body screamed with pain.

14 For a moment he could not move. The people on the bridge wondered if he was still alive. Then they saw him moving. Slowly, with great effort, he began to swim. He could not move his right arm. Still, he managed to work his way toward Cappozza.

15 By this time, another person had sprung into action. Ted Tenen worked nearby. He was in charge of the dock at the Tarrytown Boat Club. He and two other men climbed into a boat. They headed out into the river.

They reached Maria Cappozza just as Santos did. They pulled her into the boat. Then they pulled in Santos.

16 "Both were in a lot of pain," recalled Tenen. He added that Santos's back was all black and blue. "He was in so much pain I don't know how he was swimming." He added that he admired Santos for doing what he did.

17 Santos and Cappozza were taken to a nearby hospital. Although they were both injured, neither was near death. In time, they would get better.

18 Everyone was thrilled by this happy ending. And people quickly declared Santos a hero. But Santos himself did not think so. "You can call me a hero," he said. "You can call me Superman. I don't think about that stuff. I just do what I have to do."

19 Daniel Santos had shown himself to be a person of rare courage. He was willing to risk his life to help someone in need. "I really can't turn my back toward things like that," he said. "Besides, I could walk on the streets and get shot. I could die in a car accident. Life's risky; you just take that risk."

A | Finding the Main Idea

One statement below tells the main idea of the article. One statement is too general, or too broad. The other statement explains only part of the article; it is too narrow. Label the statements using the following key:

M—Main Idea   B—Too Broad   N—Too Narrow

_____ 1. Daniel Santos broke a rib when he jumped from the Tappan Zee Bridge into the Hudson River.

_____ 2. When a woman jumped off the Tappan Zee Bridge, Daniel Santos risked his life to save her.

_____ 3. Daniel Santos was willing to help a stranger one day.

Score 4 points for each correct answer.

_____ **Total Score:** Finding the Main Idea

B | Recalling Facts

How well do you remember the facts in the article? Put an X in the box next to the answer that correctly completes each statement.

1. People on the Tappan Zee Bridge were shocked when they saw Maria Cappozza

☐ a. drive in front of Daniel Santos.
☐ b. swerve her car.
☐ c. jump off the bridge.

2. After Santos saw what the woman did, he

☐ a. called 911 for help.
☐ b. jumped in the water after her.
☐ c. asked Ted Tenen to save her.

3. Ted Tenen helped by

☐ a. pulling Santos and Cappozza into a boat.
☐ b. taking Santos and Cappozza to the hospital.
☐ c. swimming out to rescue Santos and Cappozza.

4. People who learned what Santos had done said he was

☐ a. a great swimmer.
☐ b. a hero.
☐ c. an expert diver.

Score 4 points for each correct answer.

_____ **Total Score:** Recalling Facts

C Making Inferences

When you draw a conclusion that is not directly stated in the text, you are making an inference. In each group, put an X in the box next to the statement that is a correct inference.

1.

☐ a. Santos might not have lived without Tenen's help.

☐ b. Santos could easily have rescued the woman without help from Tenen.

☐ c. Tenen thought that Santos was foolish for jumping from the bridge.

2.

☐ a. No one had ever jumped from the Tappan Zee Bridge before Cappozza did.

☐ b. The Tappan Zee Bridge is the most dangerous bridge in the world.

☐ c. Santos and Cappozza were lucky to be alive after their falls.

Score 4 points for each correct answer.

_____ **Total Score:** Making Inferences

D Using Words

Put an X in the box next to the definition below that is closest in meaning to the underlined word.

1. The woman had been driving straight. But she <u>swerved</u> to miss a squirrel in the road.

☐ a. turned away from a straight path

☐ b. honked a horn

☐ c. sped up

2. The hiker felt <u>horror</u> when she saw her friend fall off the cliff.

☐ a. hunger

☐ b. anger

☐ c. great fear

3. The teen was hurt in his <u>leap</u> from the burning building.

☐ a. cry

☐ b. jump

☐ c. trip

4. Young people want to work with that trainer because she is an <u>expert</u> skater.

☐ a. not able to do something well

☐ b. tired and bored

☐ c. especially good at doing something

5. Because it had a big hole, the hot-air balloon <u>collapsed</u>.

☐ a. got bigger
☐ b. shrank
☐ c. flew away

6. The nurse was <u>injured</u> in a car crash and was taken to the hospital.

☐ a. hurt
☐ b. allowed
☐ c. seen

Score 4 points for each correct answer.

_____ **Total Score:** Using Words

E | Author's Approach

Put an X in the box next to the correct answer.

1. The main purpose of the first paragraph is to

☐ a. explain that Daniel Santos was willing to help a stranger.
☐ b. describe the trouble that Maria Cappozza was in.
☐ c. compare Daniel Santos and Maria Cappozza.

2. What is the author's purpose in writing this article?

☐ a. to get the reader to learn how to swim
☐ b. to tell the reader about the actions of a brave man
☐ c. to describe what happens when anyone falls from a bridge

3. From the statements below, choose the one that you believe the author would agree with.

☐ a. Santos is a good person.
☐ b. Santos will never try to help anyone again.
☐ c. Santos always thinks things through before acting.

Score 4 points for each correct answer.

_____ **Total Score:** Author's Approach

F	**Summarizing and Paraphrasing**

Put an X in the box next to the correct answer.

1. Which summary says all the important things about the article?

☐ a. Daniel Santos jumped 130 feet off the Tappan Zee Bridge. He was badly hurt in his fall. A passing boat picked him up. Daniel was taken to a hospital.

☐ b. Daniel Santos saw Maria Cappozza jump from a high bridge. Right away, he jumped off the bridge to save her life. Both were picked up by a boat. Many people think that Santos is a hero.

☐ c. Maria Cappozza had been a stranger to Daniel Santos. In 1996 both of them jumped off a bridge. They both were badly hurt. Both were rescued by Ted Tenen.

2. Which sentence means the same thing as the following sentence? "Water is like stone in a leap from that level."

☐ a. When you jump into water far below you, hitting the water is like hitting stone.

☐ b. Water that falls from that level is as heavy as a stone.

☐ c. When you leap from a high place, you fall like a stone into the water below.

G	**Critical Thinking**

Put an X in the box next to the correct answer.

1. Choose the statement below that states a fact.

☐ a. There should be high fences on all bridges.

☐ b. Daniel Santos was foolish to try to save Cappozza.

☐ c. Cappozza and Santos both acted quickly.

2. Santos and Tenen are alike because both

☐ a. worked at the Tarrytown Boat Club.

☐ b. were ready to help others.

☐ c. were expert divers.

3. What was the effect on Santos of hitting the water with great force?

☐ a. He broke a rib. One of his lungs collapsed.

☐ b. He was able to swim to Cappozza.

☐ c. The pain made him decide to help Cappozza.

4. In which paragraph did you find the information to answer question 3?

☐ a. paragraph 9

☐ b. paragraph 13

☐ c. paragraph 19

Score 4 points for each correct answer.

_____ **Total Score:** Summarizing and Paraphrasing

5. How is Daniel Santos an example of uncommon courage?

☐ a. Santos always makes up his mind quickly.

☐ b. Santos risked his life to help another person.

☐ c. Santos didn't tell everyone how great he was.

Score 4 points for each correct answer.

_____ **Total Score:** Critical Thinking

Enter your score for each activity. Add the scores together. Record your total score on the graph on page 115.

_____ Finding the Main Idea

_____ Recalling Facts

_____ Making Inferences

_____ Using Words

_____ Author's Approach

_____ Summarizing and Paraphrasing

_____ Critical Thinking

_____ **Total Score**

Personal Response

I wonder why _____

_____

_____

Self-Assessment

From reading this article, I have learned _____

_____

_____

A Fight for Freedom

Aung San Suu Kyi (pronounced awng sawn soo chee) didn't think she would stay in Myanmar long. She just wanted to visit her sick mother. Then she planned to return to England. That's where her husband and two sons lived. And that's where Suu Kyi, then 43 years old, had lived for the past 23 years. She had no idea that this "quick" trip in 1988 would change her whole life.

2   When Suu Kyi got to Myanmar, she saw how unhappy people were. They hated the way the government and the army ran the country. People had no rights. They had no freedom. People who spoke out were often shot. Others were tortured or thrown in jail.

3   Soon after Suu Kyi arrived, a revolt broke out. The government sent soldiers to stop it. Thousands died at the hands of the soldiers. That's when Suu Kyi knew she had to act. She had to help the people of Myanmar. Her father, Aung San, had been a great hero. In 1947 he had died helping free Myanmar (at the time called Burma) from British rule. Now Suu Kyi felt it was her turn. She decided that she, too, would fight for freedom in Myanmar.

4   Suu Kyi gave up her plans to return to England. She stayed in Myanmar. She gave speeches. She helped form a new party that stood for democracy. The people quickly grew to love and support her. But the leaders of the country did not. To them, she was nothing but trouble. They placed her under house arrest. Guards stood outside her home 24 hours a day. The guards would not let her leave and would not let anyone else visit her. They even cut her phone lines to prevent her from talking to anyone. Suu Kyi became a prisoner in her own home.

5   Even so Suu Kyi's message spread. People in Myanmar wanted to be free. In 1990 new elections were held. Suu Kyi's party won. The leaders didn't like these results, so they ignored the vote. And they kept Suu Kyi under house arrest.

6   Word of Suu Kyi's courage reached the rest of the world. In 1991 she won the Nobel Peace Prize. Now Myanmar's leaders really didn't know what to do with her. They wanted to get rid of her. But they couldn't just kill her. She was too famous for that. They offered to free her. But she had to promise to leave the country. Suu Kyi refused. She knew that if she left, the leaders would never let her back in. And she would not turn her back on the people.

Aung San Suu Kyi speaks to a group of supporters in Yangon, Myanmar, in 1997.

7   After six years, government leaders tried a new approach. They let Suu Kyi leave her house once in a while. But they said she couldn't leave the city of Yangon (formerly Rangoon). Suu Kyi refused to play by these absurd rules. Again and again, she made plans to leave the city. Each time, the army stopped her. Once she tried to leave by train. Soldiers unhooked her coach. Another time she took a car. Soldiers blocked the road. Once troops even picked up her car—with Suu Kyi inside—and turned it around to face Yangon.

8   In 1998 it happened again. This time Suu Kyi was in a van. Army troops stopped her, claiming it was "unsafe" for her to go on. For the next 13 days, she stayed in her van. The troops tried to make fun of her. They wanted people to think she was on a picnic. They set up a table with chairs. They even added a beach umbrella. They didn't fool anyone. But after nearly two weeks, Suu Kyi had to give up. She did not have enough food to last longer. And she was very sick from lack of water. She returned to Yangon, where her health improved. But again she found herself under house arrest.

9   In 1999 Suu Kyi faced a new test. Back in England, her husband was dying. He tried to come to Myanmar to see her. But the government leaders wouldn't let him into the country. They hoped his illness would drive Suu Kyi back to England. It didn't. Although she loved her husband very much, she knew he supported her work. He would not want her to quit now. So she was still in Myanmar when he died in March 1999.

10   In May 2002, government leaders began to let Suu Kyi travel more freely. They soon regretted it. Huge crowds turned out to see her wherever she went. The leaders grew nervous. The people loved Suu Kyi too much. She was too much of a threat. The leaders decided they had to stop her.

11   On May 30, 2003, Suu Kyi was in northern Myanmar. The leaders sent thugs to attack the crowd. Using clubs and sticks, the thugs beat Suu Kyi's supporters. The army admitted that four people were killed. Others claimed the death count was much higher. Dozens more were injured in the fighting.

12   Government leaders put Suu Kyi under house arrest for about four months. They said they were trying to keep her safe. But no one believes that. The leaders hid her away. They wouldn't let anyone see her. In late summer she was taken to a hospital for major surgery. In September she was returned to her home and placed under house arrest again.

13   Once again Aung San Suu Kyi has risen to the challenge. She has still not given in to her enemies. Perhaps someday she and her country will both be free. ✦

A Finding the Main Idea

One statement below tells the main idea of the article. One statement is too general, or too broad. The other statement explains only part of the article; it is too narrow. Label the statements using the following key:

M—Main Idea   B—Too Broad   N—Too Narrow

_____ 1. People in Myanmar are trying to bring freedom to their country.

_____ 2. Suu Kyi is standing against the leaders of her country to help Myanmar to freedom.

_____ 3. After Suu Kyi went home to Myanmar to help her sick mother, she made speeches.

Score 4 points for each correct answer.

_____ **Total Score:** Finding the Main Idea

B Recalling Facts

How well do you remember the facts in the article? Put an X in the box next to the answer that correctly completes each statement.

1. Before she went to Myanmar in 1988, Suu Kyi had been living in
   □ a. the United States.
   □ b. England.
   □ c. Hong Kong.

2. Suu Kyi began fighting for freedom in Myanmar after
   □ a. she won the Nobel Peace Prize.
   □ b. the leaders of the government put her under house arrest and would not let anyone visit her.
   □ c. government soldiers killed thousands of people taking part in a revolt.

3. In 1990, while Suu Kyi was under house arrest,
   □ a. she made many speeches to her people.
   □ b. her party won the elections.
   □ c. her husband died without warning in England.

4. Suu Kyi was freed from house arrest for a while, but she has been back under house arrest since
   □ a. July 1988.
   □ b. March 1999.
   □ c. September 2003.

Score 4 points for each correct answer.

_____ **Total Score:** Recalling Facts

C | Making Inferences

When you draw a conclusion that is not directly stated in the text, you are making an inference. Put an X in the box next to the statement that is a correct inference.

1.

☐ a. Not many of Suu Kyi's supporters had the courage to vote in the elections of 1990.

☐ b. The leaders of Myanmar thought that keeping Suu Kyi under house arrest would make her party lose.

☐ c. The leaders of Myanmar were proud that Suu Kyi was given the Nobel Peace Prize.

2.

☐ a. Many people in Myanmar pay attention to Suu Kyi because she is richer than the average person.

☐ b. Many people in Myanmar pay attention to Suu Kyi because she had lived in England for 23 years.

☐ c. Many people in Myanmar pay attention to Suu Kyi because she is the daughter of a national hero.

Score 4 points for each correct answer.

_____ **Total Score:** Making Inferences

D | Using Words

Put an X in the box next to the definition below that is closest in meaning to the underlined word.

1. The ship was taken by pirates, and its captain was tortured until he told them where the gold was hidden.

☐ a. made to feel pain

☐ b. made comfortable

☐ c. remembered

2. When the people learned that their king had lied to them, they joined together in a revolt.

☐ a. a group formed for the purpose of learning something

☐ b. an accident in which several people are hurt

☐ c. the action of rising up against a government

3. I can't take you seriously when you are wearing that absurd hat with feathers, fruit, and a bird.

☐ a. silly

☐ b. crisp

☐ c. needy

4. After he got sick, he regretted eating six slices of pizza, five pieces of cake, and three dishes of ice cream at the party.

☐ a. felt good about

☐ b. felt bad about

☐ c. was grateful for

5. She did not lose her purse to a smooth thief. No, this person was a <u>thug</u> who knocked her down and yanked the purse from her.

☐ a. a rough person who breaks the law

☐ b. a person who has spent some time in jail

☐ c. a person who is especially tall

6. The mayor's <u>supporters</u> cheered when he waved at them.

☐ a. people who write down what someone says

☐ b. people who dislike or work against someone

☐ c. people who agree with or back someone

Score 4 points for each correct answer.

_____ **Total Score:** Using Words

Put an X in the box next to the correct answer.

1. The main purpose of the first paragraph is to

☐ a. compare England and Myanmar.

☐ b. prove that some people who live in England are from other countries, such as Myanmar.

☐ c. make the reader want to know what happened to change Suu Kyi's life.

2. From the statements below, choose the one that you believe the author would agree with.

☐ a. The actions of a single person can make a difference in the world.

☐ b. What happens in Myanmar is not important to people outside that country.

☐ c. Might is right; that is, if you have a lot of power, whatever you do is all right.

3. Choose the statement below that is the weakest argument for awarding Suu Kyi the Nobel Peace Prize.

☐ a. She had given her people the courage to vote against their cruel leaders.

☐ b. Her father had died helping free Myanmar from British rule.

☐ c. She was giving up her own freedom to help her people gain their freedom.

Score 4 points for each correct answer.

_____ **Total Score:** Author's Approach

F Summarizing and Paraphrasing

Put an X in the box next to the correct answer.

1. Which summary says all the important things about the article?

☐ a. Since 1988 Suu Kyi has led the fight for freedom in Myanmar. She has been under house arrest most of the time and is now. Her courage earned her a Nobel Peace Prize.

☐ b. In 1991 Aung San Suu Kyi won the Nobel Peace Prize. She was living in Myanmar at the time and did not go out of the country to receive the award.

☐ c. After the leaders of Myanmar crushed a revolt in 1988, Aung San Suu Kyi led the fight for freedom in that country. Her party won the elections in 1990.

2. Which sentence means the same thing as the following sentence? "Thousands died at the hands of the soldiers."

☐ a. The soldiers used only knives, handguns, and other handheld weapons to kill people.

☐ b. Soldiers strangled thousands of people with their bare hands.

☐ c. Thousands died because of the actions of the soldiers.

Score 4 points for each correct answer.

_____ **Total Score:** Summarizing and Paraphrasing

G Critical Thinking

Put an X in the box next to the correct answer.

1. From information in the article, you can predict that

☐ a. very soon Myanmar's leaders will give up power and apologize to Suu Kyi.

☐ b. if Suu Kyi is still alive when the present leaders give up power, her people will elect her to a high office.

☐ c. the people will lose hope for change and will not care if the leaders kill Suu Kyi.

2. Suu Kyi and the present leaders of Myanmar are different because

☐ a. the leaders are fair but she is not.

☐ b. Suu Kyi is in favor of freedom but they are not.

☐ c. the leaders try to keep her safe but she takes risks.

3. What were some of the effects of Suu Kyi's efforts to leave Yangon without government permission?

☐ a. Suu Kyi refused to play by the leaders' rules.

☐ b. Troops picked up her car and turned it around; another time troops stopped her car for two weeks.

☐ c. Government leaders ignored the results of the vote in which Suu Kyi's party won.

4. In which paragraphs did you find the information to answer question 3?

☐ a. paragraphs 7 and 8

☐ b. paragraphs 8 and 9

☐ c. paragraphs 7 and 9

5. If you were a world leader, how could you use the information in the article to deal with Myanmar's leaders?

☐ a. I would not trust them.

☐ b. I would ask them for advice on running my country.

☐ c. I would suggest that they be given the Nobel Peace Prize.

Score 4 points for each correct answer.

_____ **Total Score:** Critical Thinking

Enter your score for each activity. Add the scores together. Record your total score on the graph on page 115.

_____ Finding the Main Idea

_____ Recalling Facts

_____ Making Inferences

_____ Using Words

_____ Author's Approach

_____ Summarizing and Paraphrasing

_____ Critical Thinking

_____ **Total Score**

Personal Response

A question I would like Suu Kyi to answer is "_____

_____

_____?"

Self-Assessment

When reading the article, I was having trouble with

_____

_____

Alligator Attack

An alligator similar to the one shown here attacked 14-year-old Edna Wilks in Orlando, Florida, on August 18, 2001.

Edna Wilks wanted to celebrate. She had just finished her first week of high school. So on August 18, 2001, 14-year-old Edna and five of her friends grabbed their boogie boards. They headed out for a swim in Little Lake Conway. Edna and her family had lived near this lake in Orlando, Florida, for seven years. It had always been a great place to spend time. "It's very safe," Edna said, "and we're all good swimmers."

2   Edna and her friends swam out about 30 feet. The water here was well over their heads. It was about 15 feet deep. After splashing around for a while, Edna rested on her boogie board. She let her arms hang down in the water. Suddenly she felt someone—or something—grab hold of her arm.

3   "Mark, stop playing," she said.

4   But it was not her friend Mark. When Edna looked over, she saw the head of an alligator break the surface of the water. Its jaws were shut tight on her left arm.

5   Edna said later that she didn't even have time to scream. The alligator just pulled her under.

6   The alligator began to spin around and around under the water. It dragged Edna with it. It was doing its "death roll." Edna knew the creature was trying to kill her. Suddenly Edna heard a loud crack. The alligator had snapped a bone in her arm.

7   "This is how I'm going to die," Edna thought in horror. "I'm going to drown in a minute."

8   But luckily, the alligator stopped spinning for a moment. Edna managed to stick her head above water. She gulped in air. Then, with her free hand, she tried to pry open the alligator's mouth.

9   By this time, her friends saw what was happening. Four of them began to swim away as fast as they could.

10   "Come back!" Edna cried. "Don't leave me!"

11   But the frightened teenagers were already headed to shore. Just one person stayed out in the lake with Edna. It was her best friend, Amanda Valance. Fourteen-year-old Amanda was as scared as the others. In fact, she may have been the most frightened of all. "She always said that her biggest fear was being attacked by a shark or an alligator," Edna later said.

12   Yet Amanda did not swim away. Instead, she began swimming toward Edna.

13   "For five split seconds, I felt like I had to leave," Amanda later admitted. "Then I thought, 'No, I can't leave my best friend out here to die.'"

14   As Amanda swam toward her, Edna kept trying to get her arm free. She clawed at the alligator's mouth with her right hand. She tried to dig her fingers in between its teeth. One of her fingers was badly sliced.

The rest of her hand was scratched and cut too. But at last she got the creature to open its mouth. Quickly Edna yanked her arm away from it.

15 By the time Amanda got there, blood was pouring from Edna's wounds.

16 "My arm is gone!" Edna was screaming. "My arm is gone!"

17 That was not true. Her arm was still attached. But she was too upset to realize that.

18 Amanda saw the alligator lurking just a few feet away. Its eyes seemed to watch her every move. Amanda helped Edna onto a boogie board. Then she began to move Edna toward shore. She paddled and kicked as hard as she could. At times she pushed Edna forward. At times she got in front of Edna and pulled her. In this way, she moved her friend through the bloody water.

19 Meanwhile the alligator followed close behind. Amanda feared it would attack again. She could just imagine it grabbing her feet in its awful jaws. But Amanda knew she could not give in to her fear. Her friend's life was in her hands. So she pushed aside her own fear. She tried to encourage Edna not to give up.

20 "Come on, you can make it," she kept saying.

21 As they neared the shore, the alligator finally stopped trailing them. Amanda dragged Edna the rest of the way to land. There, Edna's mother was waiting for them. The other kids had run to her house. They had told her what was happening.

22 Edna was rushed to the hospital. By the time she got there, she had lost a lot of blood. But doctors were able to save her life. They said she would recover fully.

23 Edna's mother, Nancy Wilks, was relieved. She was amazed that the alligator didn't kill Edna. "Any time you hear about an alligator attack it's usually fatal," she said. "I've never heard of anyone being pulled under and spinning and living to tell the tale."

24 Mrs. Wilks knew that Amanda was responsible. She was the one who pulled Edna to safety. Without her, Mrs. Wilks said, the alligator "would have finished my daughter off." Said Mrs. Wilks, "Edna would not be alive today if it weren't for Amanda."

25 Edna agreed that Amanda had saved her life. "She is my hero," said Edna.

26 Amanda herself was more modest about the rescue. She knew that she had to be there for Edna because, as she put it, "I couldn't see her die."

A | Finding the Main Idea

One statement below tells the main idea of the article. One statement is too general, or too broad. The other statement explains only part of the article; it is too narrow. Label the statements using the following key:

M—Main Idea   B—Too Broad   N—Too Narrow

_____ 1. An alligator attacked a swimmer and hurt her arm badly. One of her friends saved her life by pulling her back to shore.

_____ 2. A true friend is someone who helps you when you are in trouble.

_____ 3. Amanda Wilks had always been afraid of an alligator or shark attack. She almost left her friend when an alligator attacked.

Score 4 points for each correct answer.

_____ **Total Score:** Finding the Main Idea

B | Recalling Facts

How well do you remember the facts in the article? Put an X in the box next to the answer that correctly completes each statement.

1. When Edna felt something grab her arm, she thought it was
   ☐ a. an alligator chewing on her.
   ☐ b. her friend playing a trick on her.
   ☐ c. a shark trying to pull her down.

2. Alligators kill by
   ☐ a. pulling what they catch into underwater caves.
   ☐ b. shredding food into pieces as soon as they catch it.
   ☐ c. taking what they catch underwater and spinning.

3. When the alligator opened its mouth, Edna
   ☐ a. yanked her arm away from it.
   ☐ b. hit the alligator on the head.
   ☐ c. swam away and got on the boogie board.

4. The alligator stopped following Edna when she reached
   ☐ a. the hospital.
   ☐ b. the shore.
   ☐ c. her home.

Score 4 points for each correct answer.

_____ **Total Score:** Recalling Facts

C | Making Inferences

When you draw a conclusion that is not directly stated in the text, you are making an inference. Put an X in the box next to the statement that is a correct inference.

1.

☐ a. Girls are always braver than boys.

☐ b. This alligator didn't like having Edna dig her fingers between its teeth.

☐ c. Amanda didn't have any other friends besides Edna.

2.

☐ a. Alligators are not as scary as sharks.

☐ b. Edna had never known anything about alligators before the attack.

☐ c. This alligator was not afraid of humans.

Score 4 points for each correct answer.

_____ **Total Score:** Making Inferences

D | Using Words

Put an X in the box next to the definition below that is closest in meaning to the underlined word.

1. Is that a new jacket? Its price tag is still <u>attached</u>.

☐ a. ugly

☐ b. joined

☐ c. large

2. Robbers were <u>lurking</u> outside the castle one night.

☐ a. waiting and hiding

☐ b. playing games

☐ c. having a party

3. My dog was very sick. I was glad when the vet said she would <u>recover</u>.

☐ a. feel hungry

☐ b. get even sicker

☐ c. get well again

4. The star player fell down. Fans were <u>relieved</u> when he stood up and waved.

☐ a. friendly

☐ b. more nervous

☐ c. less nervous

5. Your illness is not <u>fatal</u>, so you will feel better soon.

☐ a. painful
☐ b. causing death
☐ c. well known

6. That doctor is so <u>modest</u> that he hasn't told anyone about his award.

☐ a. not proud
☐ b. pleasant
☐ c. smart

Score 4 points for each correct answer.

_____ **Total Score:** Using Words

E | Author's Approach

Put an X in the box next to the correct answer.

1 From the statements below, choose the one that you believe the author would agree with.

☐ a. Amanda Valance was a good friend to Edna.
☐ b. The alligator probably hated Edna.
☐ c. Edna is a person who takes too many chances.

2. The author probably wrote this article in order to

☐ a. describe the way an alligator kills.
☐ b. make readers afraid of swimming alone.
☐ c. tell an exciting story about a brave teen.

3. The author tells this story mainly by

☐ a. telling what happened in time order.
☐ b. comparing different ideas.
☐ c. using his or her imagination.

Score 4 points for each correct answer.

_____ **Total Score:** Author's Approach

F Summarizing and Paraphrasing

Put an X in the box next to the correct answer.

1. Which summary says all the important things about the article?

   ☐ a. Amanda Valance was Edna Wilks's best friend. Amanda didn't swim away when Edna was hurt by an alligator. Edna's mother thinks that Amanda is a hero.

   ☐ b. Edna Wilks was bitten by an alligator in a Florida lake. She finally made the alligator open its jaws. Edna made it back to the shore and was taken to the hospital. She soon recovered.

   ☐ c. Edna Wilks was swimming when an alligator closed its jaws around her arm. Edna broke free. Her friend Amanda Valance stayed with her and brought her back to shore. Amanda probably saved Edna's life.

2. Which sentence means the same thing as the following sentence? "Her friend's life was in her hands."

   ☐ a. She could save her friend's life by using her hands.

   ☐ b. Her friend's hands were very important to her.

   ☐ c. Whether her friend lived or died was up to her.

Score 4 points for each correct answer.

_____ **Total Score:** Summarizing and Paraphrasing

G Critical Thinking

Put an X in the box next to the correct answer.

1. Choose the statement below that states a fact.

   ☐ a. Alligators are cruel hunters.

   ☐ b. The alligator broke Edna's arm.

   ☐ c. Swimming is too dangerous for most people.

2. From information in the article, you can predict that

   ☐ a. Edna will save Amanda's life someday.

   ☐ b. Edna and Amanda will be friends for a long time.

   ☐ c. Amanda will no longer be afraid of alligators or sharks.

3. Amanda and Edna's other friends are different because

   ☐ a. Amanda cared about Edna but the other friends didn't care at all.

   ☐ b. Amanda is 14 years old but the other friends are younger.

   ☐ c. Amanda stayed by Edna but the other friends swam away.

4. What was the cause of Edna's terror after she opened the alligator's jaws?

   ☐ a. She thought her arm was gone.

   ☐ b. She thought her fingers had been sliced.

   ☐ c. She thought her friends had left her.

5. Which lesson about life does this story teach?

☐ a. You should never count on your friends to help you.

☐ b. Animals are often our best friends.

☐ c. Being a best friend is sometimes hard.

Score 4 points for each correct answer.

_____ **Total Score:** Critical Thinking

Enter your score for each activity. Add the scores together. Record your total score on the graph on page 115.

_____ Finding the Main Idea

_____ Recalling Facts

_____ Making Inferences

_____ Using Words

_____ Author's Approach

_____ Summarizing and Paraphrasing

_____ Critical Thinking

_____ **Total Score**

Personal Response

Describe a time when you made yourself do something that scared you.

_____

_____

_____

Self-Assessment

One good question about this article that was not asked would be "_____

_____

_____ ?"

Compare and Contrast

Pick two stories in Unit Two that tell about someone who risked his or her life to save someone else. Use information from the stories to fill in this chart.

Title	How were the rescuer and the rescued connected?	Where did each rescue take place?	How did each rescuer explain his or her reasons for acting?

If you were one of the people who were saved, what would you say to your rescuer? _____

_____

_____

UNIT THREE

In the Face of Danger

The police knew there might be trouble. That was why they put nearly 300 officers on duty. But that was really all they could do. If the Ku Klux Klan wished to come to Ann Arbor, Michigan, and hold a rally, the police had no right to stop them.

2   The Ku Klux Klan, or "KKK," has been around for years. It has a long history of hatred. Klan members hate those who are not like them. That means African Americans. It means Jews and Catholics. It also means immigrants, people from other countries who have moved here. Most people reject the KKK. They see how hateful and untrue its ideas are. But in the United States, even hateful ideas must be tolerated. Everyone has the right to think what he or she wants. And everyone has the right to free speech. So when Klan leaders asked for permission to hold a rally, Ann Arbor officials had no choice. They had to agree to it. The KKK planned to hold the rally downtown at city hall on June 22, 1996.

Keshia Thomas (lower right corner) is shown on the ground during a Ku Klux Klan meeting in Ann Arbor, Michigan.

3   Only 15 Klan members showed up. But that was enough to bring out hundreds of protesters. The protesters had the same rights as the KKK. They could shout or chant as loudly as they pleased. As the protesters marched toward city hall, they chanted, "No free speech for KKK. Let's shut them down. Let's do it today."

4   The protesters made as much noise as they could. They hoped to keep people from hearing what KKK members were saying. The plan seemed to work. KKK speakers could barely be heard. One of the shouting protesters was Keshia Thomas, an 18-year-old African American woman. She was wearing a white shirt with the letters *USA* across the front. "The KKK has every right to voice their opinions," Thomas told a reporter. "But we don't have to stand for it."

5   For a while, it looked as if the rally would end peacefully. But as the KKK members began to leave, someone in the crowd threw a rock or a stick. Others joined in. Anti-Klan protesters threw more rocks and sticks. They broke windows. One rock struck a KKK member in the head. She suffered a small cut. The police moved in quickly to control the riot. They fired tear gas into the street and arrested eight people.

6   Meanwhile a man named Albert McKeel made the crowd angry. Police later said that McKeel was not a member of the Klan. But he wore a black T-shirt with the Confederate flag on it. To the protesters, McKeel's T-shirt seemed to show that he shared at least some of the beliefs of the KKK. Several protesters crowded around him. They screamed angry words at him. "I wanted to yell at him, 'What did I ever do to you?'" said Thomas later.

7   But before she could act, a man knocked McKeel down. People began to beat him and stomp on him. "The next thing I know, this one guy hit him with a sign," said Thomas. "Then everyone else started beating him up."

8   At that moment, Thomas did an amazing thing. She fell on McKeel. But she was not trying to hurt him. She was trying to save him. Thomas shielded the man with her body and cradled his head in her arm. "Stop!" she yelled. By doing this, Thomas risked getting attacked herself. And she was protecting a man who stood for many things she hated. Thomas knew how crazy that seemed. But as she later said, "You can't kill a man for his views. Someone has got to break the cycle."

9   The police soon arrived. Officers led McKeel away from the crowd. He escaped with only a bloody nose. Thomas had surely saved him from more serious harm.

She may have even saved his life. Her bravery made Thomas famous. People across the country praised her. One newspaper wrote, "She had every right . . . to let the guy have it with her words. . . . But she knew she had no right to strike him. . . . She stood up for what was right."

10   In a letter to the editor, one woman wrote, "There is no doubt that this young woman saved the man from serious injury or death. . . . I believe that Keshia Thomas is a true American hero and is an inspiration to us all." Another woman wrote, "Here is a young woman of only 18 who could teach all races a few things."

11   Arthur Williams, Thomas's high school principal, said, "I thought it was a noble gesture on her part." He expressed pride in the fact that she stood up for what she believed in.

12   Even Jeff Berry, the KKK leader, honored her. "God bless her," he said. "She did the right thing."

13   Thomas earned several awards for her action. But she took the honors in stride. "This will all be over in a New York minute," she laughed.

14   Keshia Thomas wanted people to know that she didn't think she was really that special. "I'm no different from any other kid," she said. "A lot of kids do the right thing. They just never get the attention."

A | Finding the Main Idea

One statement below tells the main idea of the article. One statement is too general, or too broad. The other statement explains only part of the article; it is too narrow. Label the statements using the following key:

M—Main Idea   **B—Too Broad**   **N—Too Narrow**

_____ 1. Protesters at a KKK rally got out of control. They started beating a man they did not agree with. Keshia Thomas protected the man because she believed in his right to free speech.

_____ 2. Everyone in the United States has the right to speak freely. One person at a KKK rally showed that she was ready to protect that important right.

_____ 3. About 15 members showed up at a KKK rally in Ann Arbor, Michigan. Nearly 300 police were ready for them. Hundreds of protesters also came.

Score 4 points for each correct answer.

_____ **Total Score:** Finding the Main Idea

B | Recalling Facts

How well do you remember the facts in the article? Put an X in the box next to the answer that correctly completes each statement.

1. The KKK is a group that
   - ☐ a. wants to spread love.
   - ☐ b. teaches hatred.
   - ☐ c. respects all people.

2. The anti-KKK protesters wanted to
   - ☐ a. make it impossible to hear the KKK speakers.
   - ☐ b. force the KKK leaders to take back their words.
   - ☐ c. put the KKK members in jail for telling lies.

3. When protesters began to beat Albert McKeel, Keshia Thomas
   - ☐ a. shouted to the police to come quickly.
   - ☐ b. fell on top of him to protect him.
   - ☐ c. screamed angry words at them.

4. Albert McKeel suffered
   - ☐ a. a black eye.
   - ☐ b. a broken arm.
   - ☐ c. a bloody nose.

Score 4 points for each correct answer.

_____ **Total Score:** Recalling Facts

C | Making Inferences

When you draw a conclusion that is not directly stated in the text, you are making an inference. Put an X in the box next to the statement that is a correct inference.

1.

☐ a. Keshia Johnson probably did not plan on protecting a man who agreed with the KKK.

☐ b. Keshia Thomas was seriously hurt during the rally.

☐ c. Many Jews and Catholics are members of the KKK.

2.

☐ a. No police were nearby when the crowd started beating Albert McKeel.

☐ b. The KKK had never held a rally in Ann Arbor before June 22, 1996.

☐ c. Hardly anyone noticed when Keshia Thomas fell on Albert McKeel.

Score 4 points for each correct answer.

_____ **Total Score:** Making Inferences

D | Using Words

Put an X in the box next to the definition below that is closest in meaning to the underlined word.

1. Some winners simply <u>reject</u> the idea that they can lose.

☐ a. are sure about

☐ b. tell everyone

☐ c. do not accept

2. Because he was a cute baby, his family <u>tolerated</u> his crying.

☐ a. put up with

☐ b. hated

☐ c. stopped

3. At a noisy <u>rally</u> before the big game, fans showed that they stood behind their team.

☐ a. class for learning a new skill

☐ b. get-together to support a cause

☐ c. nightmare, or bad dream

4. The rally turned into a <u>riot</u> when people started throwing things and shouting.

☐ a. a coming together of family members after many years

☐ b. a polite gathering of people

☐ c. a scene of wild confusion

5. When sawing the wood, she <u>shielded</u> her eyes with plastic glasses.

□ a. protected
□ b. cleaned
□ c. shook

6. First you hit him. Then he hit you back. It's time to stop fighting and break the <u>cycle</u>.

□ a. a promise to try harder from now on
□ b. a set of events done over and over
□ c. rules for getting along with each other

Score 4 points for each correct answer.

_____ **Total Score:** Using Words

E | Author's Approach

Put an X in the box next to the correct answer.

1. What is the author's purpose in writing this article?

□ a. to get the reader to protest against the KKK
□ b. to tell the reader about a noble action
□ c. to explain the rights of U.S. citizens

2. Choose the statement below that best describes the author's opinion in paragraph 2.

□ a. The KKK is a force for peace in the United States.
□ b. No one should belong to the KKK.
□ c. What the KKK teaches makes a lot of sense.

3. The author tells this story mainly by

□ a. using his or her imagination.
□ b. comparing different points of view.
□ c. telling about events in the order they happened.

Score 4 points for each correct answer.

_____ **Total Score:** Author's Approach

F Summarizing and Paraphrasing

Put an X in the box next to the correct answer.

1. Which summary says all the important things about the article?

☐ a. Keshia Thomas was one of the protesters at a KKK rally in Michigan. The crowd attacked a man they thought agreed with the KKK. Thomas bravely protected him and his right to free speech.

☐ b. Police had to permit a KKK rally in Ann Arbor, Michigan. The rally turned ugly when people started throwing rocks and sticks. Keshia Thomas was one of the protesters. She showed great courage.

☐ c. The KKK is a group that is against many people. Even though Keshia Thomas did not like what the KKK teaches, she protected it with her life. For that, she is a hero.

2. Which sentence means the same thing as the following sentence? "'This will all be over in a New York minute,' she laughed."

☐ a. She said, "This will be all over New York soon."
☐ b. She said that the excitement would be over very soon.
☐ c. She said, "This won't be done for a long time."

Score 4 points for each correct answer.

_____ **Total Score:** Summarizing and Paraphrasing

G Critical Thinking

Put an X in the box next to the correct answer.

1. Choose the statement below that states an opinion.

☐ a. Police say that McKeel was not a KKK member.
☐ b. McKeel should not have worn that T-shirt to the KKK rally.
☐ c. One KKK member suffered a cut when a rock hit her in the head.

2. Keshia Thomas and KKK leaders are alike because

☐ a. they gave long speeches in front of crowds.
☐ b. they may have saved Albert McKeel's life.
☐ c. both believe they have the right to free speech.

3. What was the effect of the flag on Albert McKeel's T-shirt?

☐ a. It made the protesters angry at McKeel.
☐ b. It made people throw rocks at a KKK member.
☐ c. It made the police fire tear gas into the crowd.

4. In which paragraph did you find the information to answer question 3?

☐ a. paragraph 5
☐ b. paragraph 6
☐ c. paragraph 7

5. How is Keshia an example of uncommon courage?

☐ a. She put herself in danger to protect someone else.

☐ b. She believes in free speech for all Americans.

☐ c. She wore a white shirt with the letters *USA* across the front.

Score 4 points for each correct answer.

_____ **Total Score:** Critical Thinking

Enter your score for each activity. Add the scores together. Record your total score on the graph on page 115.

_____ Finding the Main Idea

_____ Recalling Facts

_____ Making Inferences

_____ Using Words

_____ Author's Approach

_____ Summarizing and Paraphrasing

_____ Critical Thinking

_____ **Total Score**

Personal Response

How do you think Albert McKeel felt when Keshia Thomas shielded him? _____

_____

_____

Self-Assessment

While reading the article, _____

_____

was the easiest for me.

Risking It All

The storm began suddenly. It started with rain. Then the rain turned to ice and snow. The wind gusted to 80 miles an hour. By late afternoon on September 25, 2000, the blizzard was in full force. It was the worst storm in New Zealand's Kaimanawa Ranges in years.

2   Brian Pickering had just set out on an eight-day hike through these mountains. He had not expected a blizzard. Still, he was not too worried. Fifty-two-year-old Pickering knew what he was doing. He had studied this trail carefully. There was a hut just three miles away. He figured he could wait out the storm there.

3   As Pickering trudged along, he saw footprints in the snow. Two people were up ahead of him. At last he spotted them. A 42-year-old man named John Painting and his 13-year-old son Matthew had collapsed on the trail.

4   "They obviously weren't in a good way," recalled Pickering. In fact, both father and son had hypothermia. This means that their body temperatures

---

John Painting (second from left) and his son Matthew (right) meet with the rest of their family after their scare in the Kaimanawa Ranges.

were dropping. Their minds had become slow and confused, and they had lost most of their energy. Now they were too weak even to walk.

5   Pickering gave them some chocolate from his pack. They could barely eat it. "It certainly didn't look good for them," he later said.

6   At that point, Brian Pickering faced a choice. The smart thing, perhaps, would have been to keep walking toward the hut. That was the only safe place to be in such brutal weather. Pickering could have wished these strangers good luck, left them some extra food, and said goodbye.

7   But Pickering didn't do that. He refused to walk away and leave the two hikers to die. Instead, he decided to stay and help them. He knew the blizzard could kill all three of them. But that was a chance Pickering was willing to take.

8   He got out his tent and tried to set it up. The wind whipped it out of his hands. So Pickering opened the Paintings' sleeping bags. He got John and Matthew to crawl into them and wrapped a sheet of plastic around them. Then he dug his cell phone out of his pack.

9   In most places on this trail, a cell phone would have been useless. The high mountains blocked radio signals. But Pickering was lucky. Here the cell phone worked. He dialed 111, the New Zealand version of 911.

10 Rescue workers were ready to help. They knew it wouldn't be easy. Still, a search-and-rescue team headed out. They didn't get far. They couldn't see a thing. And the wind was so strong that it snapped their heads back. One 220-pound rescuer was picked up by a gust of wind and thrown 65 feet through the air. The team tried to crawl on their hands and knees. But soon it was clear to everyone that until the storm let up, Pickering and the Paintings were on their own.

11 As darkness settled in, Pickering did everything he could to keep the Paintings alive. He fed them nuts and chocolate and tried to warm them with his own body heat. Most of all, he tried to keep them awake. He knew that if they fell asleep, they would die. "I had to yell at the top of my voice," he said. "I tried to ask Matt about school and John what he did. But you couldn't hear anything above the howling wind."

12 Meanwhile the police and rescue workers could only wait for the weather to improve. "We sat here in absolute despair," said police officer Cliff Jones. Once an hour, Jones called Pickering on his cell phone. Each time Pickering sounded weaker and weaker. Clearly, hypothermia was beginning to have an effect on him too.

13 Jones knew Pickering might not survive the night, and Pickering also realized it. "I could hear it in his voice," said Jones. "It was gut-wrenching stuff."

14 Jones urged Pickering to hang on, to keep fighting for his life.

15 "I'll do my best," Pickering promised.

16 Then, at 3:30 A.M., Pickering's cell phone batteries wore out, and the phone went dead.

17 By this time Pickering was really struggling. He knew there was another cell phone in one of the packs. It was only 15 feet away from him, but he didn't have the strength to walk over and get it. He just wanted to sink into sleep, yet somehow he fought off that urge. Slowly . . . slowly . . . he crawled toward the pack. It took him four hours, but at last he reached it. He took out the phone and called Cliff Jones. He reported that he and the Paintings were still alive.

18 As morning dawned, a second rescue team set out. The blizzard was still raging. But at 10 A.M. this team reached the hikers. They set up tents. They gave hot food and dry clothes to Pickering and the Paintings. Eventually the three hikers perked up. It took another 24 hours for rescue helicopters to make it in. But at last, on September 27, everyone was flown to safety.

19 Cliff Jones was thrilled by the happy ending. And he marveled at Pickering's courage.

20 "I simply cannot say enough about the human qualities of the man," said Jones. "It took an enormous amount of bravery to stay with those people, knowing he might not make it through the night himself."

21 As Jones said, "He put his life on the line for those people." ✐

A Finding the Main Idea

One statement below tells the main idea of the article. One statement is too general, or too broad. The other statement explains only part of the article; it is too narrow. Label the statements using the following key:

M—Main Idea   B—Too Broad   N—Too Narrow

_____ 1. The blizzard of September 25, 2000, had 80-mile-per-hour winds and heavy snow. The wind was strong enough to pick up a 220-pound man.

_____ 2. A blizzard in the mountains can kill hikers who are not prepared. Sometimes it takes courage and skill to survive such a blizzard.

_____ 3. A skilled hiker found two hikers in trouble during a blizzard. At great risk to himself, he kept them safe until help arrived.

Score 4 points for each correct answer.

_____ **Total Score:** Finding the Main Idea

B Recalling Facts

How well do you remember the facts in the article? Put an X in the box next to the answer that correctly completes each statement.

1. The Kaimanawa Ranges are in

☐ a. New Zealand.
☐ b. New Guinea.
☐ c. New Mexico.

2. Someone who has hypothermia has

☐ a. a bad stomachache.
☐ b. a low body temperature.
☐ c. trouble breathing.

3. Brian Pickering used the cell phone to call

☐ a. rescue workers.
☐ b. the Paintings' family.
☐ c. his own family.

4. To reach his other cell phone only 15 feet away, Pickering crawled for

☐ a. one full day.
☐ b. ten minutes.
☐ c. four hours.

Score 4 points for each correct answer.

_____ **Total Score:** Recalling Facts

C | Making Inferences

When you draw a conclusion that is not directly stated in the text, you are making an inference. Put an X in the box next to the statement that is a correct inference.

1.

☐ a. Brian Pickering was well prepared for a hike in the mountains.

☐ b. The Paintings had not brought any useful hiking gear with them.

☐ c. The Paintings did not want to go to the hut three miles away.

2.

☐ a. The second rescue team got through just because they were braver than the first team.

☐ b. Anyone who goes to sleep in the Kaimanawa Ranges will die.

☐ c. Brian Pickering thought that chocolate and nuts made good hiking snacks.

Score 4 points for each correct answer.

_____ **Total Score:** Making Inferences

D | Using Words

Put an X in the box next to the definition below that is closest in meaning to the underlined word.

1. Two tired hikers <u>trudged</u> up the steep hill.

☐ a. ran quickly

☐ b. walked slowly

☐ c. skipped happily

2. <u>Obviously</u> hungry, the little birds again opened their mouths wide when their mother returned.

☐ a. clearly

☐ b. barely

☐ c. for the first time

3. Which <u>version</u> of the story do you like better, the book or the movie?

☐ a. form

☐ b. rules

☐ c. color

4. The score was 10-0 in the last two minutes of play. You could see the <u>despair</u> on the faces of the players on the losing team.

☐ a. smiles of joy

☐ b. playful look

☐ c. lack of hope

5. More than three years passed. <u>Eventually</u> people forgot about the crime.

☐ a. after a while
☐ b. suddenly
☐ c. in spite of

6. The tourists <u>marveled at</u> the beauty of this building.

☐ a. were troubled by
☐ b. were bored by
☐ c. were amazed by

Score 4 points for each correct answer.

_____ **Total Score:** Using Words

E Author's Approach

Put an X in the box next to the correct answer.

1. The main purpose of the first paragraph is to

☐ a. describe the Kaimanawa Ranges.
☐ b. introduce the reader to Brian Pickering.
☐ c. tell how bad the blizzard was.

2. Choose the statement below that best describes the author's opinion in paragraph 7.

☐ a. Pickering did not know that he was putting himself in danger. Otherwise, he would have left the Paintings and gone on alone.
☐ b. Pickering knew the risk he was taking, and he accepted it.
☐ c. Pickering was willing to help the Paintings, but only if he could be sure that both he and they would survive.

3. The author probably wrote this article in order to

☐ a. tell the reader about Pickering's courage.
☐ b. tell how rescue workers do their jobs.
☐ c. describe what happens when people get hypothermia.

Score 4 points for each correct answer.

_____ **Total Score:** Author's Approach

F | Summarizing and Paraphrasing

Put an X in the box next to the correct answer.

1. Which summary says all the important things about the article?

   ☐ a. A hiker and his son collapsed in the Kaimanawa Ranges. A blizzard raged around them for two days. On September 27, 2000, they were rescued.

   ☐ b. Rescue workers found hikers Brian Pickering, John Painting, and Matthew Painting barely alive. The three hikers helped each other survive a mountain blizzard.

   ☐ c. During a blizzard in New Zealand's Kaimanawa Ranges, Brian Pickering found two hikers who were close to death. Risking his own life, he kept them alive for two days until rescuers reached them.

2. Which sentence means the same thing as the following sentence? "He refused to walk away and leave the two hikers to die."

   ☐ a. He decided to walk away from the two hikers, even if it meant they might die.

   ☐ b. He could not leave the two hikers there to die, so he stayed with them.

   ☐ c. The two hikers refused to walk away from him, knowing that they would die alone.

   ```
   Score 4 points for each correct answer.

   _____ Total Score: Summarizing and Paraphrasing
   ```

G | Critical Thinking

Put an X in the box next to the correct answer.

1. Choose the statement below that states a fact.

   ☐ a. People who are in trouble in New Zealand dial 111.

   ☐ b. The Paintings should not have been hiking on the mountain during a blizzard.

   ☐ c. Pickering was a better hiker than the Paintings were.

2. From information in the article, you can predict that

   ☐ a. Pickering will avoid other hikers from now on.

   ☐ b. the Paintings will probably not hike in the mountains when storms are expected.

   ☐ c. no one will sign up to work on rescue teams in New Zealand because it is too dangerous.

3. Pickering was not able to set up a tent. What was the cause of this problem?

   ☐ a. It was snowing too much.

   ☐ b. The wind was too strong.

   ☐ c. Pickering felt too cold.

4. How is Brian Pickering an example of courage?

   ☐ a. He was a skilled hiker who had studied trail maps and knew the trail well.

   ☐ b. He recognized the signs of hypothermia and knew what to do to keep people warm.

   ☐ c. He remained with the Paintings and helped them survive, even though he knew staying might kill him.

5. How could you use the information in the article to hike safely in the mountains?

☐ a. I would tell the police every time I began a long hike.

☐ b. I would check the weather forecast before beginning a long hike.

☐ c. I would not carry anything but chocolate and nuts with me.

Score 4 points for each correct answer.

_____ **Total Score:** Critical Thinking

Enter your score for each activity. Add the scores together. Record your total score on the graph on page 115.

_____ Finding the Main Idea

_____ Recalling Facts

_____ Making Inferences

_____ Using Words

_____ Author's Approach

_____ Summarizing and Paraphrasing

_____ Critical Thinking

_____ **Total Score**

Personal Response

What was most surprising or interesting to you about this article?

_____

_____

Self-Assessment

One of the things I did best when reading this article was

_____

I believe I did this well because _____

_____

A Close Call

It was supposed to be a night of fun. And at first, it was. Dozens of teenagers streamed into the Wedgwood Baptist Church on Wednesday, September 15, 1999. Seventeen-year-old Mary Beth Talley came. So did her friend, 18-year-old Heather MacDonald. In all, more than 125 people showed up for this youth rally in Fort Worth, Texas.

2 Early in the evening, a rock band took the stage. Loud music filled the air, and the teenagers loved it. Most of them sat in the front of the church. That's where Heather MacDonald was sitting with her mother, Laura. Heather had been born with Down's syndrome. People with Down's syndrome learn more slowly than others. Mary Beth Talley stood in the lobby and handed out programs to people who came late.

3 As the band played, a stranger walked through the outer door of the church. He wore jeans and a dark jacket. That was fine because no one had to dress up to come to the rally. But this man was smoking a cigarette. Smoking is not allowed in the church. So a janitor walked over to the man. Politely the janitor asked Larry Ashbrook to put out his cigarette. That's when 47-year-old Ashbrook went crazy. He pulled out a gun and began shooting.

4 Mary Beth Talley did not see the janitor die. She was in a different part of the lobby. But she heard the shots. She knew something terrible was happening. At that point, she could have run to safety. She could have rushed out of the church or hidden in one of the offices down the hall. But she didn't. She ran into the main part of the church where the band was playing.

5 "There's a man shooting outside!" she screamed over the music.

6 To the people at the rally, this did not seem possible. Many of them thought it was an act. The program said a skit would be performed later in the evening. People figured this was the start of that short play. Mary Beth knew better. She had a role in the skit. She knew the script did not call for a crazed gunman.

7 Despite their disbelief, people began to crouch down on the floor.

8 "We all got down," said 12-year-old Caleb Payne, "but we didn't know what was happening. We thought it was a skit . . . we thought we would play along."

Mourners gather at a memorial in front of the Wedgwood Baptist Church in Forth Worth, Texas.

9 Mary Beth looked over at Heather MacDonald. Heather was making no effort to hide. She was still sitting up. Mary Beth ran over to her.

10 "Laura," she said to Heather's mom, "there is a guy with a gun. We need to get down."

11 Together, Laura and Mary Beth tried to get Heather down on the floor. But Heather was confused. She didn't understand why she had to move. Besides, Heather didn't like small, tight places. She didn't want to be jammed down between rows, so she resisted. She fought the attempts to push her to the floor.

12 Suddenly Larry Ashbrook burst into the room and began to fire bullets at the stage. The band members quickly ran for cover. Then Ashbrook walked up and down the aisles, shooting wildly. Many people still thought this was part of the skit and that Ashbrook was an actor shooting blanks or paintballs. Because they were all ducking down, they couldn't see that people really were being wounded and killed.

13 Mary Beth knew it was real, and she also knew she was not well hidden. Ashbrook could easily see her. "My body was in full view of him," she later said. Yet she stayed where she was, using her body as a shield to protect Heather MacDonald.

14 It didn't take long for Ashbrook to spot her. When he saw her, he walked over and pointed his gun at her. Mary Beth felt a sharp sting as a bullet ripped through her back.

15 "Was I just shot?" she thought. Later she said, "I thought it would hurt a lot, but it really didn't. I guess I was numb."

16 Even when she realized she had been wounded, Mary Beth did not move. She did not let go of her friend. As blood oozed from her body, she kept rubbing Heather's arm. "I just kept saying to Heather, 'You've got to be quiet and stay down with me,'" she later recalled.

17 After shooting Mary Beth, Ashbrook moved away. He kept firing bullet after bullet. It seemed like the gunfire would never end. "I looked straight down most of the time," Mary Beth said. "After I was shot, I kept thinking, 'Keep breathing, keep breathing, keep your eyes open, keep Heather calm.'"

18 At last the nightmare ended. Larry Ashbrook turned the gun on himself and took his own life. By then seven innocent people lay dead, and seven more were wounded.

19 Mary Beth heard people around her shouting, "He's dead! He's dead!" At last she released her grip on Heather MacDonald. She dragged herself out of the church and collapsed on the ground. Rescue workers rushed her to the hospital.

20 Mary Beth Talley survived her gunshot wound. When asked about what she had done, she shrugged it off. "I just did what needed to be done," she said. "I was taught to put other people first."

21 But Laura MacDonald had a different opinion. "Mary Beth will not accept the title," she said, "but she is a real hero."

A | Finding the Main Idea

One statement below tells the main idea of the article. One statement is too general, or too broad. The other statement explains only part of the article; it is too narrow. Label the statements using the following key:

M—Main Idea   B—Too Broad   N—Too Narrow

_____ 1. No one thought that a church rally would be dangerous. However, the rally at Wedgwood Baptist Church turned deadly when a stranger came in.

_____ 2. More than 125 young people came to a rally at Wedgwood Baptist Church on September 15, 1999. When a man with a gun started shooting, people thought it was part of a skit.

_____ 3. At a church rally, a gunman killed seven people. One teenager shielded her friend from the bullets. She herself was shot but survived.

Score 4 points for each correct answer.

_____ **Total Score:** Finding the Main Idea

B | Recalling Facts

How well do you remember the facts in the article? Put an X in the box next to the answer that correctly completes each statement.

1. Mary Beth knew something bad was happening when she
   - ☐ a. heard the gunshots.
   - ☐ b. saw the stranger walk through the church's outer door.
   - ☐ c. saw that Heather was sitting upright.

2. Most people crouched down on the floor because
   - ☐ a. they thought the gunman would kill them.
   - ☐ b. they wanted to play along with the skit.
   - ☐ c. they were trying to protect each other.

3. When Mary Beth and Laura tried to get Heather to crouch down, Heather
   - ☐ a. began to scream loudly.
   - ☐ b. quickly lay down and put her arms over her head.
   - ☐ c. fought against them.

4. Mary Beth shielded Heather until
   - ☐ a. Ashbrook was dead.
   - ☐ b. Ashbrook walked away from them.
   - ☐ c. the rescue workers came to get her.

Score 4 points for each correct answer.

_____ **Total Score:** Recalling Facts

C | Making Inferences

When you draw a conclusion that is not directly stated in the text, you are making an inference. Put an X in the box next to the statement that is a correct inference.

1.

☐ a. No one could get into the rally without an invitation.
☐ b. Heather's mother did not trust Mary Beth.
☐ c. Heather could be stubborn at times.

2.

☐ a. Mary Beth helped to plan and run the rally.
☐ b. Heather would have agreed to crouch down if she had known Mary Beth better.
☐ c. The gunman shot only those people whom he knew and disliked.

Score 4 points for each correct answer.

_____ **Total Score:** Making Inferences

D | Using Words

Put an X in the box next to the definition below that is closest in meaning to the underlined word.

1. At special classes, the young man learned about the machines a janitor uses to take care of a building.

☐ a. person who decorates a room or building
☐ b. another name for a school principal
☐ c. person who takes care of and cleans a building

2. Study the script I have given you. Go over your lines until you know them by heart.

☐ a. the written words of a play
☐ b. clothes that actors in a play wear
☐ c. the things on a stage where a play is given

3. The robber resisted for a long time, but police were finally able to bring him into the station.

☐ a. wrote his own life story
☐ b. fought against something
☐ c. helped bring someone to justice

4. First my legs were numb, but then I started feeling them again.

☐ a. without any feeling
☐ b. not able to move
☐ c. very warm

5. A little bit of blood <u>oozed</u> from the cut all night, so I changed the bandage.

☐ a. dried up
☐ b. flooded
☐ c. came out slowly

6. Rob caught the fish and then <u>released</u> it into the lake.

☐ a. captured
☐ b. let go
☐ c. tightened the grip on

Score 4 points for each correct answer.

_____ **Total Score:** Using Words

E | Author's Approach

Put an X in the box next to the correct answer.

1. The author uses the first sentence of the article to

☐ a. suggest that the night might not have been fun.
☐ b. describe the teenagers who came to the church rally.
☐ c. compare the church rally and a rock concert.

2. The main purpose of the first paragraph is to

☐ a. tell how Mary Beth Talley saved the life of her friend Heather MacDonald.
☐ b. explain to the reader how even a church rally can be dangerous.
☐ c. tell who was at the rally and when and where it took place.

3. Choose the statement below that best describes the author's opinion in paragraph 4.

☐ a. Mary Beth was easily frightened, and she sometimes frightened others too.
☐ b. Mary Beth was so confused that she did not know that she should run away from danger.
☐ c. Mary Beth thought it was more important to help others than to keep herself safe.

Score 4 points for each correct answer.

_____ **Total Score:** Author's Approach

F | Summarizing and Paraphrasing

Put an X in the box next to the correct answer.

1. Which summary says all the important things about the article?

☐ a. Larry Ashbrook came to a church rally in Texas. When the janitor asked him to put out his cigarette, he pulled out a gun and began to shoot wildly.

☐ b. Heather MacDonald, a teen with Down's syndrome, did not like small places. She refused to crouch down on the floor when a stranger began shooting. People around her thought the man was acting in a skit.

☐ c. An angry stranger began shooting at a teen rally at a Texas church. Mary Beth Talley shielded a friend. The gunman shot Talley and then killed himself. Talley and her friend survived, but seven others died.

2. Which sentence means the same thing as the following sentence? "And when asked about what she had done, she shrugged it off."

☐ a. When people asked her about what she did, she acted as if it was nothing special.

☐ b. She could barely remember what she did, so she only shrugged when people asked her about it.

☐ c. It bothered her when people asked her about what she did, and she refused to answer.

Score 4 points for each correct answer.

_____ **Total Score:** Summarizing and Paraphrasing

G | Critical Thinking

Put an X in the box next to the correct answer.

1. Choose the statement below that states a fact.

☐ a. A church is not the proper place for a rock band to perform.

☐ b. The janitor should not have asked the man to put out his cigarette.

☐ c. The gunman shot Mary Beth in the back.

2. Mary Beth and Heather are different because

☐ a. Heather wanted to hide but Mary Beth did not think hiding was helpful.

☐ b. Heather was sitting at the front of the church but Mary Beth was standing in the lobby.

☐ c. Mary Beth saw the janitor get shot but Heather did not see it.

3. The stranger became angry and started shooting. What was the cause of his anger?

☐ a. Someone had told him to change his clothes.

☐ b. The janitor had asked him to put out his cigarette.

☐ c. Mary Beth would not give him a program for the rally.

4. In which paragraph did you find the information to answer question 3?

☐ a. paragraph 3

☐ b. paragraph 4

☐ c. paragraph 12

5. If you were in charge of a teen meeting, how could you use the information in the article to keep out anyone who might make trouble?

☐ a. allow people to smoke cigarettes

☐ b. have the meeting in a small meeting room

☐ c. invite only the people you knew well

Score 4 points for each correct answer.

_____ **Total Score:** Critical Thinking

Enter your score for each activity. Add the scores together. Record your total score on the graph on page 115.

_____ Finding the Main Idea

_____ Recalling Facts

_____ Making Inferences

_____ Using Words

_____ Author's Approach

_____ Summarizing and Paraphrasing

_____ Critical Thinking

_____ **Total Score**

Personal Response

If you could ask the author of the article one question, what would it be? " _____

_____

_____ ?"

Self-Assessment

I can't really understand how _____

_____

_____

Alone Against the Tanks

The trouble in China began quietly. On April 15, 1989, Hu Yaobang had a heart attack and died. He had been a popular Chinese leader. People had liked him because he tried to soften the harsh rule of the Communist Party. That party ruled the country. But in 1987, the party had fired him. Now, upon hearing that he had died, thousands of students took to the streets of Beijing, a city in the People's Republic of China, to honor him.

2   They laid flowers in Tiananmen Square. The square is a huge open space in the heart of the city. The first day, thousands of students showed up, and even more came the next day. Soon workers and children joined the students. By the middle of May, more than one million people were jammed into the square. Many came to stay. Living in tents, they set up a city within a city. They even put out their own newspaper.

3   These people started out to honor Hu. But soon their gathering turned into a protest. People were unhappy with Communist rule. They didn't want to overthrow it. But they did have some demands. They wanted more freedom. They wanted their leaders to be more honest and less corrupt. The students also wanted less crowded classrooms and cleaner housing.

4   As the days passed, the people grew bolder. They sang songs and marched through the square shouting their demands. They carried signs that expressed their desire for more freedom. The signs sent the party a message. The people wanted more say in what their leaders did.

5   For weeks Communist leaders did not respond. They hoped the protesters would get tired and go home. At last, on May 20, party officials ordered people to leave the square. But thousands refused to budge. Art students even built a 30-foot white statue of a woman holding a torch and called it the "Goddess of Democracy." It looked like the Statue of Liberty. Many people had their photos taken next to it.

6   Party leaders were not happy. On June 2 they sent 8,000 soldiers to clear the square. When a huge force of students and workers blocked their way, the soldiers didn't know what to do. But the now-angry leaders did. On the night of June 3, party officials ordered tanks into the square. They told the soldiers to shoot and kill if necessary.

A young man blocks the path of four government tanks in Tiananmen Square in Beijing, China, on June 5, 1989.

7   The next morning, soldiers in an armored car ran over a man. His death enraged the protesters. They raced after the car on bicycles. When they caught up with the car, they set it on fire. They also beat up the soldiers.

8   The army struck back hard. Soldiers opened fire on the crowd outside the square, killing hundreds. The protesters fled in fear. But they didn't quit. They regrouped and marched against the tanks again. Once more the soldiers opened fire.

9   One man who was helping the wounded held up his arms. "See the blood of the Chinese people on my hands!" he cried. The soldiers paid no attention. Over the next few hours, they drove everyone away. The once-full square became empty except for the soldiers and their tanks.

10   By the next morning it looked as though the protesters had been permanently silenced. The government sent more tanks to keep the peace. A column of 17 tanks was moving down a road toward the square. Then, out of nowhere, came one man. He wore long pants and a white shirt. In his hand he carried what looked like a shopping bag. This man walked out in front of the leading tank and stood there. He didn't scream or jump up and down or make angry moves. He just stood quietly—one man against all those tanks.

11   The line of tanks came to a stop. When the lead tank moved to the left, the man moved the same way. When the tank moved back to the right, the man moved back as well. This dance lasted more than a minute.

12   Then the man scrambled up onto the tank. He said a few words to the driver. Only he and the driver know exactly what he said. But it was reported that he said something like, "Why are you here? My city is in chaos because of you."

13   Right after that, three fellow protesters came to help the man. They pulled him from the tank before soldiers could hurt him. The man then walked away and disappeared from view.

14   Who was this man? No one knows. Some people thought they recognized him, but nothing was proven. "Who he was is not important at all," said Han Dongfang, a protest leader. "What is important is that he was there. By his act he gave encouragement to a lot of people."

15   This one unarmed man stood up against the power of the Communist Party. He became a symbol of freedom around the world. His likeness appeared on T-shirts and posters. He was praised in a song and a movie. *Time* magazine even named him one of the top 20 leaders of the 20th century.

16   What happened to the man? Some think he was killed by party leaders. Others do not agree. But no matter what happened to him, one thing is clear. This man left an image of courage that will live on for years.

A | Finding the Main Idea

One statement below tells the main idea of the article. One statement is too general, or too broad. The other statement explains only part of the article; it is too narrow. Label the statements using the following key:

M—Main Idea   B—Too Broad   N—Too Narrow

_____ 1. When people see that change is needed, they find ways to get that message to their leaders. A huge crowd at Tiananmen Square told Communist leaders that people wanted change.

_____ 2. Angry crowds in Beijing demanded changes to Communist rule. After soldiers killed many of the protesters, one man dared to face a line of tanks alone. His courage made him famous.

_____ 3. In May 1989 more than one million people gathered in Beijing's Tiananmen Square. Communist Party leaders sent 8,000 soldiers to break up the crowd. One man stood up to the army tanks.

Score 4 points for each correct answer.

_____ **Total Score:** Finding the Main Idea

B | Recalling Facts

How well do you remember the facts in the article? Put an X in the box next to the answer that correctly completes each statement.

1. At first people gathered at Tiananmen Square to
   - ☐ a. honor a leader who had died.
   - ☐ b. protest the firing of Hu Yaobang.
   - ☐ c. work to overthrow the Communist Party.

2. By the middle of May, the crowd in the square numbered
   - ☐ a. about 8,000.
   - ☐ b. about one million.
   - ☐ c. about 100 million.

3. Art students built a statue that looked like
   - ☐ a. the leader of the Communist Party.
   - ☐ b. the Chinese leader Hu Yaobang.
   - ☐ c. the Statue of Liberty.

4. The unknown man who stood before the tanks
   - ☐ a. said something to the tank driver and then left.
   - ☐ b. shouted angry words and shook his fist at the tank driver.
   - ☐ c. carried a sign that said "Give Me Democracy or Give Me Death."

Score 4 points for each correct answer.

_____ **Total Score:** Recalling Facts

C | Making Inferences

When you draw a conclusion that is not directly stated in the text, you are making an inference. Put an X in the box next to the statement that is a correct inference.

1.

☐ a. The man who stopped the tanks was probably a member of the Communist Party.

☐ b. Most likely, the party was afraid that the protesters were getting too strong.

☐ c. The Communists did all they could to avoid killing any of the protesters.

2.

☐ a. Han Dongfang knew the name of the man who stood before the line of tanks.

☐ b. The unknown man was sure that the tanks would not run him over.

☐ c. The driver of the first tank could have run the man over if he had chosen to.

Score 4 points for each correct answer.

_____ **Total Score:** Making Inferences

D | Using Words

Put an X in the box next to the definition below that is closest in meaning to the underlined word.

1. Your enemies had some <u>harsh</u> words to say about you.

☐ a. kind
☐ b. cruel
☐ c. careful

2. A group of rich families planned in secret to <u>overthrow</u> the king and set up their own leader.

☐ a. read a report to
☐ b. throw a party for
☐ c. put out of power

3. The <u>corrupt</u> official would break any law for money.

☐ a. not honest
☐ b. faithful
☐ c. special

4. The dwarf <u>enraged</u> the giant by stealing his gold.

☐ a. pleased
☐ b. bothered
☐ c. angered

5. The classroom was in <u>chaos</u> after 20 white mice escaped from their cages.

☐ a. a state of quiet and peace
☐ b. a lack of order
☐ c. the action of repeating something

6. Who painted the <u>likeness</u> of George Washington that is on the U.S. dollar bill?

☐ a. picture
☐ b. president
☐ c. money

Score 4 points for each correct answer.

_____ **Total Score:** Using Words

E | Author's Approach

Put an X in the box next to the correct answer.

1. The main purpose of the first paragraph is to

☐ a. tell the reader that April 15, 1989, was a quiet day.
☐ b. describe the life of the Chinese leader Hu Yaobang.
☐ c. explain why students crowded the streets of Beijing.

2. What is the author's purpose in writing this article?

☐ a. to get the reader to be against the Communist Party
☐ b. to tell about one man's stand against a cruel government
☐ c. to entertain the reader with personal details about a well-known hero

3. The author tells this story mainly by

☐ a. describing events in the order they happened.
☐ b. comparing and contrasting different ideas.
☐ c. using his or her imagination.

Score 4 points for each correct answer.

_____ **Total Score:** Author's Approach

F | Summarizing and Paraphrasing

Put an X in the box next to the correct answer.

1. Which summary says all the important things about the article?

☐ a. In June 1989 Chinese people demanded changes, but soldiers broke up their protest. A man who stood alone before a line of tanks became a symbol of freedom.

☐ b. In 1989 a man walked onto Tiananmen Square. He stood before a line of tanks. For a minute, he moved back and forth so the tanks could not get around him.

☐ c. In 1989 the People's Republic of China was ruled by the Communist Party. Not all Chinese were happy with the party. They gathered to protest in Beijing.

2. Which sentence means the same thing as the following sentence? "By the next morning it looked as though the protesters had been permanently silenced."

☐ a. When they woke up the next morning, the protesters decided that they had been silent too long.

☐ b. The next day, it seemed as if the protesters were going to stay quiet from now on.

☐ c. The protesters could no longer hear anything when they woke up the next morning.

Score 4 points for each correct answer.

_____ **Total Score:** Summarizing and Paraphrasing

G | Critical Thinking

Put an X in the box next to the correct answer.

1. Choose the statement below that states an opinion.

☐ a. Hundreds of protesters died when the soldiers opened fire on them.

☐ b. The man who faced the tanks was the bravest of all.

☐ c. On June 2 party leaders sent 8,000 soldiers to clear the square.

2. Han Dongfang and the man who faced the tanks are different because

☐ a. Han Dongfang's name is well known but no one knows the other man's name.

☐ b. the unknown man was brave but Han Dongfang showed no courage.

☐ c. Han Dongfang was unhappy with the Communists but the other man agreed with them.

3. On June 4 soldiers in an armored car ran over a man in the square. What was the effect of his death?

☐ a. Party leaders decided to clear the square.

☐ b. The protesters became very angry.

☐ c. People set up tents in the square.

4. In which paragraph did you find the information to answer question 3?

☐ a. paragraph 4

☐ b. paragraph 7

☐ c. paragraph 9

5. Which lesson about life does this story teach?

☐ a. Might makes right.

☐ b. Crime does not pay.

☐ c. Every person counts.

Score 4 points for each correct answer.

_____ **Total Score:** Critical Thinking

Enter your score for each activity. Add the scores together. Record your total score on the graph on page 115.

_____ Finding the Main Idea

_____ Recalling Facts

_____ Making Inferences

_____ Using Words

_____ Author's Approach

_____ Summarizing and Paraphrasing

_____ Critical Thinking

_____ **Total Score**

Personal Response

Why do you think the unknown man stood up against the tanks? _____

_____

_____

Self-Assessment

From reading this article, I have learned _____

_____

_____

Compare and Contrast

Pick two stories in Unit Three that tell about someone who faced an attack from another person or other persons. Use information from the stories to fill in this chart.

Title	How did the attack begin?	Who was hurt or killed in the attack?	What effect did the brave person's actions have?

Of the topics mentioned in these stories, I would like to learn more about _____

_____

_____

Comprehension and Critical Thinking Progress Graph

Directions: Write your score for each lesson in the box under the number of the lesson.
Then put a small X on the line directly above the number of the lesson and across from
the score you earned. Chart your progress by drawing a line to connect the Xs.

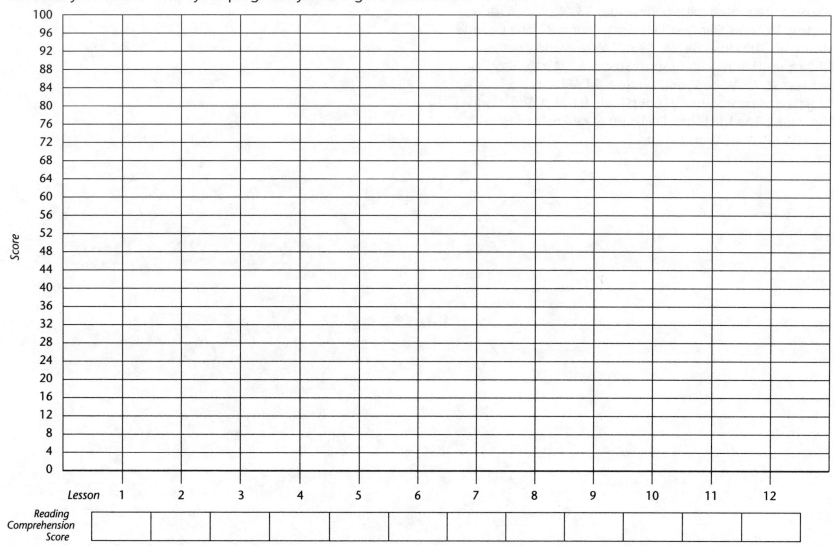

301020

Photo Credits